Dear Pat & Joe,

Thank you for your Passion
and your Presence.

WISHING YOU ALL THE
BLEST +

Billy ⁊

THE NOW-IST

FINDING THE SIGNS

TO YOUR ULTIMATE DESIRES

IN NO TIME

BILLY MANDARINO

BALBOA.
PRESS
A DIVISION OF HAY HOUSE

Balboa Press books may be ordered through booksellers or by contacting:

Balboa Press
A Division of Hay House
1663 Liberty Drive
Bloomington, IN 47403
www.balboapress.com
1 (877) 407-4847

Print information available on the last page.

ISBN: 978-1-5043-9694-3 (sc)
ISBN: 978-1-5043-9696-7 (hc)
ISBN: 978-1-5043-9695-0 (e)

Library of Congress Control Number: 2018901409

Balboa Press rev. date: 04/04/2018

"Time is what keeps the light from reaching us. There is no greater obstacle to God than time."

— Meister Eckhart

TABLE OF CONTENTS

CHAPTER 1

THE NOW-IST SYMBOL

---❖---

"Be still, and know that I am God."

— Psalm 46:10

One of my favorite books of all time is Paulo Coelho's *The Alchemist*, which has been translated into sixty-nine languages. It is a brilliant tale of a shepherd boy, Santiago, in search of buried treasure. He does not know what the treasure is or if he will be able to surmount the obstacles along the way. A journey that starts out seeking worldly goods turns into a discovery of the treasure found within.

This truly is every person's story. We are all out seeking to make it in the world. We are all trying to create a life that will fulfill our needs, wants, and desires, focused mainly on a world of form and recognition. I was this boy most of my life, until an event occurred that changed my "Personal Legend" as it is called in *The Alchemist*. A Personal Legend is your life's spiritual purpose. It is a spiritual calling that awakens a deep desire and passion to live with a sense of purpose for something greater than yourself.

Not that many years ago, I was blessed with a satori (a flash of enlightenment). This awakening started a most-unexpected path for my life. The spiritual hunger I experienced was voracious. Since this light-filling event, my days have been made up of 90 percent spirit and 10 percent worldly duties. As I ascend on this journey, the increase in synchronistic events is mind-blowing! When you align with your highest calling, God sends you all that you will need to fulfill it. You will not have to try to be,

1

this or that, or create more abundance through effort and striving. Your life becomes a great series of magical and incredible events that you can share with the world, through inspiration and actualization.

One day I was walking down the hallway of the condominium building my family and I lived in and thought, *I looked down to look up.* I know that sounds confusing. It was to me at first as well, as I stared with shock and awe at the carpet I had walked on for years each and every day. The carpet throughout the entire building's hallways was covered with a life-fulfilling image. Days after my flash of enlightenment on the golf course in Santa Barbara (you will discover this in the GOLF chapter), I noticed a design image in the carpet that stopped me in my tracks. The symbol is now the cover of this book. It is the most evolving and inspiring symbol I have ever seen or experienced in my entire life. As I studied it for months, deeper and deeper meaning continued to flow into my very being. I know this must sound crazy or outlandish. Please suspend your disbelief and read this account with the eyes of a child in imagination or as if you were watching a movie.

As I stared at the image, the first thing I noticed was a figure floating above the earth. (Look at this symbol now and many times throughout the expressing and impressing of the following words.) Not only was there one being above the planet, but there were four of them. They all had their arms outstretched and hovering above the bright, shining sphere of light. This was amazing to me because my satori was the exact same experience. I was shot from earth! I was rocketed above the planet and floating in space, marveling at the light around the earth. This phenomenal image that I was staring at was the perfect symbolic representation of the life-changing event I'd just encountered! I have experienced countless forms of synchronicity in my life. Never before had one this profound hit me right between the eyes. The feeling of floating I experienced in my initial flash of peace and knowing was represented in this sign/symbol of confirmation. I later learned the power of this experience and what that floating meant for the highest part of me. Neville Goddard's (DeVorss Publications 1941) powerful and inspiring book *Your Faith is your Fortune* explains this phenomenon precisely.

Floating

To rise to the level of any state, is to automatically become that state in expression. But in order to rise to the level that you are not now expressing, you must completely drop the consciousness with which you are now identified. Until your present consciousness is dropped, you will not be able to rise to another level. Do not be dismayed. This letting go of your present identity, is not as difficult as it might appear to be. The invitation of the scriptures, 'to be absent from the body and be present with the Lord' is not given to a select few. It is a sweeping call to all mankind. The body from which you are invited to escape, is your present conception of yourself, with all of its limitations. While the Lord with whom you are to be present, is your awareness of being. To accomplish this seemingly impossible feat, you take your attention away from your problem and place it upon just being. You say silently but feelingly, 'I Am'. Do not condition this awareness but continue declaring quietly, 'I am, I am.' Simply feel that you are faceless and formless and continue doing so until you feel yourself floating. Floating is a psychological state, which completely denies the physical, through practice in relaxation and willfully refusing to react to sensory impressions. It is possible to develop a state of consciousness of pure receptivity. It is a surprisingly easy accomplishment. In this state of complete detachment, a definite singleness of purposeful thought can be indelibly engraved upon your unmodified consciousness. This state of consciousness is necessary for true meditation. This wonderful experience of rising and floating is the signal that you are absent from the body, or problem, and are now present with the Lord.

The next thing that came to my awareness was the oneness. As you look at all of the Now-ist symbols, they are connected to one another continuously with no lack of continuity. Each symbol simply connects naturally and effortlessly to the next. It is like we are all in the universe depicted as this vast stretch of carpet. While we are all connected in oneness, we also have an individual "I am" presence. When I first realized this, it was years after walking the hallways each and everyday. This symbol just keeps unfolding deeper and deeper meanings to me. It conditions and reminds me, through a type of meditation with a shape and form, to stay in the present moment always.

The Sacred Labyrinth Walk is the ancient practice of "circling to the center" by walking the labyrinth. It redirects your focus on self-alignment. Labyrinths have been in use for more than four thousand years. Their basic design is fundamental to nature and many cultures and religious traditions. Whatever one's religion, walking the labyrinth clears the mind and gives insight.

I am instantly transformed into the image I am watching as I walk. My attention places me above the planet and connects me to my Higher-Self. This is usually the first "step" I take when I begin the walk. I often recite Psalm 46:10 as I enter this awareness. "Be still, and know that I am God." Making this pronouncement connects me to the light of that oneness. In addition, I imagine the letter *k* is removed from the word *know*. This creates the word *Now*. "Be still, and *now* I am God." Herman Melville's famous quotation "God's one and only voice is silence," rings true to this point. To be still, or silent, means God is talking to you. The walking meditation stills my mind and directly connects me to the present moment. This silence is the key to release and relaxation. Resistance cannot exist in this state of being. The day's problems and stress melt away when I am connected to this truth.

The symbol continues to unfold its hidden meanings as I meditate on it while walking. I see the center of the symbol depicting the earth and the light of the world. You can see this light radiating outward to the person floating or hovering above it. This to me is the most powerful aspect of the Now-ist symbol; it states in form and image, "I am the light of the world. Again Jesus spoke to them, saying, 'I am the light of the world. Whoever follows me will not walk in darkness, but will have the light of life,'" (John 8:12).

Later, Jesus states in Matthew 5:14, "You are the light of the world." The divine power and presence of this realization lifts us all to the rightful awareness Jesus is calling each one of us to. You can say "I am the light of the world," and not feel blasphemous. Jesus tells us, "I am the light of the world," and "You are the light of the world." I AM is the name of God that was told to Moses thousands of years ago. This is a towering truth that most people walk through their everyday lives completely oblivious to. The absolute power in those words should change your life forever! "But everything exposed by the light becomes visible, for everything that is illuminated becomes a light itself." (Ephesians 5:13). The apostle Paul writes these words to remind us of the universal abundant power of the light. The Now-ist symbol comes from a Catholic origin. The word catholic means "universal." My intention is to inspire all humankind to remember the existential truth this symbol conveys.

The cross is the central image of the Now-ist symbol. Traditionally, it is used as a reminder that Jesus died on the cross for all of us. I am inspired to express the power of this symbol, as it displays the omniscient now. Notice how a cross is made of one line that is vertical and another that is horizontal. Consider that the vertical line represents a line going straight up to Heaven, a representation of divine time. The horizontal line is a "time line" of ordinary or chronological time. The moment these two lines intersect is where I would like your awareness and attention to go Now. When you take divine time and cross it with chronological time that is the Now! For example, you could be going throughout your day, a full schedule of appointments in time and have no awareness of the present moment. When you stop and breathe, in a meditative or prayerful manner, surrendering to the moment, you have entered the divine time. You have in effect, crossed your linear time with divine time and entered the Now.

As you become aware of this inspiring truth about the cross, look at the Now-ist symbol again. You can clearly see that the center of the symbol has a bright light in it. This is where I imagine the crossing of divine and chronological time, creating an explosion of light sign, which renders symbolic awareness to this revealed truth. This point of intersection is the catalyst for the symbol's transforming awareness. It is there to remind us all, through its design, shape, and form- "I am the light of the world." Pay very close attention to the symbol as a whole. You can now look at the Now-ist symbol and see this image, as it omnipotently expresses its secret. Billions of people look at the cross and imagine a dead Jesus, who has suffered physically and bled for our sins. Most have a feeling of sadness and guilt. It reminds us of this event in time and place which focuses on the past. Nowhere in scripture does Jesus ever say, I am the crucifixion. He does, however, state in John 11:25, "I am the resurrection and the life.

The one who believes in Me, even if he dies, will live." This is the hope and inspiration for the entire world.

The soulful revelation you experience when you deeply understand this truth- "I am the light of the world," will change you forever. Look at the symbol and meditate on this image of light. You now see the light emanating from the world and you as the light of the world. You see you, replicated as light rays, shooting out all around the light. The center represents the light and the world all in one. Every time I see the Now-ist symbol, I silently say to myself, "I am the light of the world." It is the ultimate call to us all. "I am" is the name of God. It fills me instantly with the powerful truth of who I am. "I can do all things through Christ who strengthens me." (Philippians 4:13). I feel this truth and never allow doubt or any other contrary event or opinion to hold sway on my highest self.

I will stand over the Now-ist symbol in the hallway and realize… I am standing over me, looking at me, as the light of the world. It is this duality of being that we all must bridge and connect to our true-self. As we go out into the world, we pass signs, symbols, and synchronistic reminders daily. Our awareness of being and true strength is zapped by the inertia of living. If you can say and most importantly feel, "I am the light of the world," nothing will be impossible to you, ever! When this all-satiating reality settles into you, you feel the divine power that was given to you at birth, as the operant power in your life. This becomes the nucleus of your existence. Lahiri Mahasaya, (1828-1895) immortal for his order of self-realization and philosophy of Kriya Yoga, encourages us with these wise words, "Seek Divine wealth, not the paltry tinsel of earth. After acquiring inward treasure, you will find that outward supply is always forthcoming." This seems like a divine technology to me. When you place your attention only on the divine wealth, which is your true self, that focus and resonance elevates your life. It transforms you into all forms of abundance and treasures. The alchemy that takes place is the formula for turning base metal into gold!

The world famous, quest-adventure-fantasy genre told by Paulo Coelho in *The Alchemist* is the story of all mankind. We all venture out into the world to find treasure and great riches. The guiding power most frequently used is the thinking mind. It reacts to the circumstances the journey presents to us. We become discouraged and lost due to this erroneous focus of mind. The grand climax to the tale brings our main character back home to where he began his adventure- only to find that his greatest treasure was located right where he began! When you live each day with your awareness, intention, and declaration of being "the light of the world," you enter a place that is closer than near and sooner than now.

The Now-ist symbol is that reminder daily, to be that light of the world in every moment. As I walk the halls of the building that I live in, I "look down to look up," every single day. Walking and looking at the symbol reminds me to stay present and imagine my divine self above the planet. While I am up there, above my problems and conflicts, all is peace and oneness with the source of all, God. I am free of the mind and the mind-made delusions. I feel like the main character in Coelho's *The Alchemist*. I align with the young shepherd who strikes out into the world to find his "Personal Legend" which is, our life's spiritual purpose! It is a spiritual calling that awakens a deep desire and passion to live with a sense of purpose for something greater than yourself. I have walked these hallways for years and never noticed the Now-ist symbol right below my feet. My ambitious proclivity and sense of having to do and to be was the counter intuitive practice that kept my focus away from the Now. Heavenly-granted, just like the beloved character in the story acquires, my true treasure was home with me all along.

And so is it, with you, my dear reader. The power you seek is right there within you. The journey you take is not an outward-bound adventure. Most of us tend to constantly stay in the seeking mode of life. We think the circumstances of life are the grade by which we measure our success or failure. The great teacher of the Now, Eckhardt Tolle, expresses this point beautifully, "Life will give you whatever experience is most helpful for the evolution of your consciousness. How do you know this is the experience you need? Because this is the experience you are having at the moment." What if we stopped judging what presents itself in our lives, and paid greater attention to the reason it was there? What if we took full responsibly for it and no longer felt like a victim of circumstance? How would your life journey change course and lead you in the direction of your awakened self? These are the questions you should ask yourself, especially when your journey has you lost in a forest of debris. The guidance you seek is just a small step in the direction of you. It almost sounds too simple to be true. Yet, you are the "gold" you have been seeking after. We are encouraged by the Psalmist in chapter 118 verse 22, "The stone the builders rejected has become the cornerstone." You are that stone. No longer do you need to reject your common self and think you have to seek to find the cornerstone of your faith. You are the "I Am that I Am." You are the very thing that you have been searching for all this time. Look no further; the search is over. You are the light of the world, and nothing you ever do or say can change this truth of your very being. Love that light, never question it, or doubt it. The didactic Taoist aphorism, "A journey of a thousand miles begins with a single step," is your reminder to stay present, here, now. I encourage you to take that first step inward, toward the you that you are seeking.

CHAPTER 2

NOW...WON

"There can be only one." — *Highlander*

I remember being in high school and watching the movie *Highlander* for the first time. It was late at night and I was alone. The VCR tape was loaded and I sat on the couch at my dad's house in complete darkness for a moment, as I waited for the movie to begin. Surrounded by the black and taking a deep breath in the silence, something happened inside me, that I would not discover until years later. *I was present and content* wanting for nothing and truly free of time. The moment only lasted for a few minutes, but it tethered me to the Now for the first time. I now know it was a sign of what was to come. With the spark of a cinematic, imaginative soul-filling-musical-ode to the NOW, I was captivated by the theme of this story.

The main character is taken through time as an immortal being that cannot die. He was chosen hundreds of years earlier during a battle where he was injured so badly he should have died. The villagers were shocked and dismayed that he was on death's door and the next day is fresh and healthy as if the battle wounds had never occurred. Ousted from the village after being stoned and beaten, the crowds shouted, "He has the devil in him."

Alone and wandering, he meets his teacher and master of the immortals. The great teacher had been seeking him to teach him the ways of the chosen ones.

He explains his gift to him. Ultimately, all the immortals will be drawn to a faraway land and the final two will battle to the end. "For there can be only ONE."

The only way for an immortal to perish is to separate the head from the body. Therefore, a sword is the only weapon carried by all the gifted ones.

The brilliant spiritual teacher Neville Goddard makes this powerful observation about the speed in which the "cutting off" from worldly thinking can change your life. "When the truth comes into the world, he comes not to bring peace but a sword. He is going to separate you from that traditional background that enslaved you in the past. Because real progress in this world, religious progress, is a gradual transition to a God of experience. For you experience God and the whole thing reflects it."

Goddard further shares his powerful inspiration of the now. "If right now, you reflect upon your life and say within yourself, I wouldn't want to live this again, then you'd better start changing it because I can make you a promise. Your next life is this life. If you cannot now in reflection say, I desire to live it again, then start today to lay down new tracks. For you stand in the presence of energy and you can't stop walking. The curvature of time will bring you back and back and back forever and forever until you break it. Then you awaken and enter a circle of awakened humanity."

The head is the thinking mind's carriage. Jesus was crucified at Golgotha, translated "the place of a skull." In the story *Highlander*, the immortals cut off the heads of the other immortals in pursuit of the great prize. I find the symbolism here perfect for the action of cutting off all resistance to the oneness of the Now. It is the thinking mind and the negative thought forms conjured up with circumstance that are the head's undoing. When an immortal is finished off, all his powers become one with the victor. The low energy falls away and the high energy lifts up the one who is advanced. This all may sound harsh and crude to you. However, it was my first glimpse of a parable about the Now.

An elk stag is on the beach next to the Highlander. He is encouraged by the master to feel the stag's heartbeat to become one with that heartbeat and to merge with the energy of the elk. He begins to feel the synchronicity with the stag's heart and runs quickly and powerfully just like the animal. He is told that this is called the "Quickening." When you become one with your surroundings and merge with what life gives you in the present moment, your being-ness travels from nowhere to NOW-here.

Once, for a short period of time, I felt the erratic beating of my own heart. At night as I lay in bed, I felt short rushes of beats and then nothing.

I could feel the pace skipping and sometimes even stop altogether. This concerned me as heart issues had been known to occur in my family's history. My grandfather, the patriarch of our family, passed away very young from a massive heart attack. These kinds of thoughts would enter my mind and fear and worry attempted to assail me.

Golfing one day during this time, a vascular surgeon "coincidentally" was paired up with me. After playing a few holes, I discovered what line of work he was in. He vehemently insisted that I go to the Urgent Care right after the round. Doing as he instructed, the male nurse (whose name was *Jaime*, the same middle name as my brother, *a sign*) confirmed that the EKG showed my heart was going on runs.

Driving home from that visit, I had a flash of the *Highlander* movie. The "Quickening" was a state in the story where the immortal was elevating his awareness to oneness of present moment energy with the stag elk. Maybe this variable heartbeat had a higher purpose to get my attention and look within my heart to find the answers. (I am not suggesting that you don't seek professional assessment when experiencing chest pain or erratic heartbeat.)

I am sharing my experiences and truths. My innermost calling is talking here and Now. As a Now-ist, I have learned to always pay attention, be astonished, and tell other people. My heart, the most powerful source of energy in our bodies, was talking to me directly trying to get my undivided presence to convey a very specific message. It then occurred to me to enter the Now, fully and meditatively. To do this, I had to strip away the vail of thinking and surrender to the feeling part of awareness. As I deeply became one with my heart and breathed into it, the answers were revealed. I took my pulse before entering the present moment, then after. The variable heartbeat (Tachycardia as the medical profession identifies it) was all over the map. Once I detached from the thinking mind and was truly "up there" in present moment awareness, my heart rate became steady as a drumbeat in perfect time.

Dog...God

The Heart Math Institute in northern California has conducted some amazing studies on the connection between humans and their pets. One study fitted a boy and his dog with heart rate monitors. When the boy entered the room where his dog was waiting and consciously felt feelings of love and genuine care for his pet, both entered a state that is known as entrainment of the heart (becoming one heartbeat and feeling the rhythm of that shared pace.) The EKG graph showed the same pattern as his pet when the boy felt these feelings without even physically touching the dog.

My heart's awakening to the similar entrainment was revealed through synchronized awareness to the variable heartbeat that I was experiencing. I feel and more importantly believe, the "Quickening" I was merging with was God's high awareness energy field. This enlightenment is my felt oneness with being. Thus changing my heart rate to sync with the higher speed of the divine. I have always believed that God's unconditional love is simply emulated in the love and caring of a dog. After all, *Dog* spelled backwards is *God*.

Won-ness

To be *One* is to stay connected to the oneness of all that is. The most famous line from *Highlander* is "There can be only one!" He never aged a day in hundreds of years. He lived each day in the same manner as all the days, seeking to battle with other immortals until just one was left. I find the battle we all face is similar to the Highlander's battle. Negative thoughts, worried or stress-filled emotions, these are the foes of everyday life. Continuously, ordinary and common place are the fights in our heads, taking us out of the present moment awareness. The NOW can never be WON if we are always defeated by the world of the thinking mind. The anagram in the word *Now* is the great secret of the Now-ist. *Now* spelled backwards is *Won*. When one lives constantly in the Now, one has Won the great prize of Oneness.

The late great Prince, one of the most talented artists to ever walk this planet, once said, "I only live in the now; I think it keeps you young." His ability to immerse himself in music was the greatest display of musical presence I have ever encountered. He played many different styles of music (40 different instruments) as if he were the music! He truly lived each note, each word, each emotion the given song had to offer. I am inspired by his example of being a Now-ist. Witnessing his live concerts confirmed he never strayed from his present moment awareness in his music. Spiritually, Prince was a man of God. His faith was well chronicled throughout his incredible career. The power of the Now has been well documented in many studies, ranging from a significant increase in the body's immune system to stress decimation, enhanced relationships, greater productivity, more prosperity and the list could go on and on.

Once I read the *Power of Now* by Eckart Tolle, my third eye was opened to the Now. The book literally found me. I was a new property manager and eager to start growing my business, taking on all the odd jobs this new profession offered. One day I was cleaning out a very cluttered and messy, one bedroom condo. After hours of dust and mounds of minutia, I opened the hall closet that was loaded with books. You see, this property was to be lightly furnished not a hoarder's delight. I had such a short amount of time to get this unit on the market for rent that I was not thinking clearly. I filled three large, blue recycling containers full to the brim with all the books. Sweating profusely, I rolled each overly stuffed container to the trash/ recycling room. On the last trip down the long hallway, feeling exhausted, I closed the door behind me and started to walk back to the unit. After about three steps, I heard a loud slap on the floor. In my mind, I figured some books had fallen out of the bins. As I opened the door and peered inside, *The Power of Now* by Eckart Tolle was face up and looking right at me. A couple hundred books were in these bins, yet this was the only book to crash to the floor and call me back inside. I remembered hearing about this book on a TV show months before. I felt strangely drawn to it and flipped through its silverfish-eaten pages. The previous owners of this book had marked it up with ideas, underlines, dog ears, and applications to their own life's situations. There must have been three different owners because I identified a variety of colored pens and pencils making notes. I took it home and read it very slowly and deliberately. I did not really understand what he was talking about until the third reading in its entirety. Then I had a satori! This flash of enlightenment you will read about in the GOLF chapter.

I know we are all guided. I love these comforting words from *A Course in Miracles*, "If you knew who walked beside you at all times, on the path that you have chosen, you could never experience fear or doubt again." We must pay attention to the signs that show up in our daily lives. Most of us think and react to happy accidents or joyful coincidence as just funny happenstance. I have always had a spiritual hunger and a healthy imagination for the unknown. When life shows me an event that is extraordinary, I pay attention and open all my senses. It is in our awareness that the growth is found. Our moments of decision shape our being-ness. This simple little spark of enlightenment has taken me to Oscar Wilde's vantage point: "We are all in the gutter, but some of us are looking at the stars."

Ephesians 4:4-5, 10 reads "There is one body and one Spirit, just as you were called to one hope when you were called; one Lord, one faith, one baptism; one God and Father of all, who is over all and through all and in all. He who descended is the very one who ascended higher than all the heavens, in order to fill the whole universe." Oneness... it is all we have. In deep-rooted truth and freedom in being, this is the immortal truth of us all. The Ephesians' verse tells us in grand sincerity to be one is to be whole. When you are in oneness, you are content and at peace. Every aspect of your life is complete: emotionally, socially, physically, spiritually, financially and in all totality. We all come from oneness and all of us will return to oneness. I am here to tell you- you do not have to die to return to that oneness. You want to die to the past or to the future every single moment you live. When you are in the NOW, you have WON! This has become my ultimate calling and life's mission to share this great truth. I am a Now-ist and that is the great secret to joy, health, abundance, peace, and freedom.

You may be saying to yourself, this is too simplistic and elementary. How can all of my problems, worries, fears, and lack be solved by becoming a Now-ist? Ask yourself this question: *Has everything that has ever happened in my life ever occurred at a time other than the now?* The answer is very easy to come up with- isn't it? You see, human beings have a need to feel like they have left a trace. Some kind of trail behind them to let everyone else know they were here. This is imprinted in our minds and hearts early in life. We are told to stand out from the crowd. Make your mark on the world. Be better than the others in your class or group. This can be all well and good, even great sometimes. The problem arrives with the identification of being better or worse than the others. The memory stores that positive or negative feeling and we stack those on each other until we live our lives in a reverse order far more than the here and now. The future then becomes the focus when the past leaves us wanting. Our peers, family members, and contemporaries can make an identity for us, if we do not have present moment awareness.

The Word

John 1:1, "In the beginning was the Word, and the Word was with God, and the Word was God." The power of one word. It can conjure up feelings, images, sensory perception, emotions, memories, and much more. If I asked you: What does *Fear* mean to you? You could instantly come up with an account, memory, or total recall of a moment in your life to convey that emotion. The word *Hate* can bring most to a feeling of intensity in the mind and body rather quickly. To ask someone what the word *Love* truly means to them might be the simplest reaction to a single word in the human language. We all experience and feel *Love* from the moment we are born. Our recollection is natural and instinctual to the word. Perhaps this word is the most popular word in the entire human language. After all, it is written in 1 John 4:8 "God is *Love*." I am also inspired by these words, "Love is the reduction of the universe to a single being," from Victor Frankel, an extraordinary survivor of the Holocaust.

Allow your imagination to see the whole universe for a moment. Feel the immensity in that concept. The vast and unfathomable universe. As I drift in my being to see the universe in my mind's eye, an awesome, overwhelming, all encompassing presence comes over me. I then zoom at a very high rate of speed from that infinity to the top of planet earth. Hovering up there in the silence and stillness for a moment, I look down, and clearly see myself standing on the ocean's shore. I have just experienced what Frankel described as *Love*. I am *One*. Just *One* being in the vast universe, standing on the shore.

When I am here, *Now*, completely present in the moment that is the power of *One*. That Being, completely still and silent on the seashore, is when you have *Won*. I discovered the greatest secret of my life. This truth rushed over me like a new birth of being, the first time it happened to me… When you are in the NOW, you have WON, NOW spelled in reverse is *WON*.

I learned that my higher self is up above the planet and my lower self is standing on the shore. The great power in the *Now* is simple, yet deeply complex for the thinking mind to surrender to. Endless tangents and scenarios are the mind's best friends to combat the *Now*…

- "My calendar is way too full. I can't do all that."
- "How can I get to fifteen different appointments in a work day?"
- "I have too much month left at the end of money."
- "My kid had better get home by midnight!"

Stress! This is the *Now's* nemesis. Thinking you are much more than that moment. People live that feeling each and every day thousands of times, never quite happy enough. Time is running out! Got to get to that meeting, appointment, babysitter, store, with so much to do! The *Now* does not live in time. It is eternal and infinite. I have studied many accounts of people, like you and me, experiencing heaven during a near death experience. They all have come back with the same awareness of no time in heaven. Only the eternal *Now*. Many have said everything is happening at once. They could see their entire life as one *Now* moment.

I AM Imagination

One of my favorite spiritual teachers is Neville. This divine soul was prolific during the 1940s and 50s. Many considered him to be a prophet. He spoke with such wisdom and truth about the power of your imagination. Moved by his inspiration, I would like to share an incredibly powerful passage from his book, *Immortal Man*. I find this to be the best representation of this essential message to you.

If you know that your own wonderful human imagination is God, you cannot fail in achieving your objectives. 'All things are possible to him who believes.' In that statement, Mark equates man with God. For with God, all things are possible. In Matthew, the story is told of a rich young man who wanted to enter the kingdom of heaven. Jesus said, 'Sell all you have and follow me.' But the rich man was disheartened because he had so many possessions. Then Jesus said, 'It is easier for a camel to pass through the eye of the needle than a rich man to enter heaven.' His disciples asked, 'Who then can be saved?' He answered, 'With men it is impossible, but with God all things are possible'. With men and women who do not know who they are. That is what he means. With men and women that do not know the lord's name. First, I must know his name. 'For those who know the name put their trust in thee. For thou oh Lord would not forsake those who seek thee.'

Let us look for his name as revealed in scripture. Moses said to God, 'If I go to the Israelites and I say to them, that the God of your forefathers has sent me to you, and they say to me. 'What is his name?' What shall I say? Then God said to Moses, 'Say I Am, that is who I Am. Say, I Am hath sent you, fore that is my name forever and forever and by this name I shall be known through out all generations. I have no other name.' Just be aware. To be aware is to say, I Am. Without uttering a sound, by just being aware, that I-Am-ness is God. That's what I mean by Imagination.

What is *Faith*? We are told in the eleventh chapter of Hebrews, "Faith is the assurance of things hoped for, the evidence of things not seen. By faith we understand that the world was created by the word of God. So that things which are seen were made out of things that do no appear, and without faith, it is impossible to please him. He calls a thing that is not seen as though it were, and the unseen becomes seen." Having found that God is my own wonderful human *Imagination*.

How would I go about creating something that seems either difficult or impossible? Naturally I start with God. The most blessed gift in the world is a strong vivid imagination. A clear idea and a determinant vision of things as I would like them to be. Then in my mind I conjure a scene, which would imply the fulfillment of my dream. See it clearly, give it all the tones of reality, as much sensory vividness as I can, and believe in that imaginal act. Have it so fixed in my mind, that I am oblivious to all things round about me that would deny it. Then walk in the assumption it is so. Assume the feeling of the wish fulfilled and simply ignore everything denying it. Then I am calling a thing that is not now seen, as though it were seen, and that unseen state will become seen.

I tell you, I know this from my own experience. It never fails. But we are the operant power. Knowing what to do is one thing, but doing it is another.

Will you do it? To know is all well and good, but will you do it? Those who know thy name put their trust in thee. I may be a shock to the whole vast world, but I cannot avoid telling the story. I have experienced it. I can only share with you what I know, and I am telling you, that if you dare to assume the feeling of the wish fulfilled and walk in the assumption that it is so. Ignoring the senses, ignoring the facts of life that deny it. In a way that you do not know. It will become a reality in your world.

IMAGINATION. Like Neville conveys, I too believe, it is one of God's greatest gifts. Using one's imagination is an underrated tool. Imagination harnesses power of divine manifestation in all time and space. Albert Einstein, arguably the most brilliant thinking mind to walk the planet tells us, "Imagination is more important than knowledge. For knowledge is limited to all we now know and understand, while imagination embraces the entire world, and all there ever will be to know and understand."

God is hidden in the word Imagination. The *Sign* of our Oneness with God has always been there right in front of us. The contraction of the words *I AM* is *I'M*. I and M are the first two letters in *Imagination*. Therefore, God is in Imagination and God is Imagination itself.

The name of God is I AM.

How many times a day are these words uttered in all the languages of the earth?

I am poor.
I am lonely.
I am sad.
I am broken.
I am lost.
I am not enough.
I am a loser.

We are all numb to the drone of common-place, daily minutia. Our attention can easily be taken from us. Our presence is lost in all forms of media, news, doing, and keeping up, or not keeping up with the Jones. Our I AM's must be the main focus of our daily self talk. The Now-ist awareness is the most important divine presence we feel. For when we are in the Now, we are experiencing the connection to the heavenly realm of timelessness and eternal oneness.

CHAPTER 3

THE ART OF CONNECTION...
ATTRACTING YOUR FUTURE NOW

―――✿―――

"Learn how to see. Realize that everything
connects to everything else."

— Leonardo Da Vinci

There is an ancient story in the Buddhist tradition that offers up a great teaching on the power of connection, or in this case, disconnection. For in order to know what you want, it is important to know what you do not want. Buddha was well-known for his ability to respond to evil with good. There was a man who knew about his reputation and he traveled miles and miles to test Buddha. When he arrived and stood before Buddha, he verbally abused him, he insulted him, and he challenged him; without letting up, he did everything he could to offend Buddha. Buddha was unmoved. He simply turned to the man and said, "May I ask you a question?" The man responded, "Well, what?" Buddha said, "If someone offers you a gift and you decline to accept it, to whom then does it belong?" The man replied, "Then it belongs to the person who offered it." Buddha smiled, "That is correct. So if I decline to accept your abuse, does it not then still belong to you?" The man was speechless and walked away.

The energy that connects us all is magnetic. Not only do we connect to people and things, we attract into our lives the energy of the like energy. Like attracts alike. In the above story of Buddha, he did not judge the man that was causing the abuse. He was completely impenetrable. His enlightened presence and Now-ist mentality simply redirected the energy of abuse back to the source of the abuse. He did not become attached to a victimized focus of, "Poor me, why am I getting berated by this person?" Instead, he uses the power of his awareness to remain calm and present, authentic to his highest self. His reaction can be likened to a Kung Fu master that redirects the opponent's force back into the opponent. He does not take on the impact of the blow. Since he does not offer any resistance, it is impossible to connect with that energy. How would most of us react to a strong verbal assault? Typically, our egos would instantly come to fight and defend the onslaught of offensive comments and words. Consequently then, momentum and inertia can take you over, if you are not present and aware of your true-self.

All too often, we allow ourselves to erroneously connect to what we do not want. Perhaps, it is our desperate need to connect with others and find communion that causes this behavior. We can all recall moments in time that places us in a situation contrary to our desires. A harsh reality of this is the victimized person that stays in a volatile or abusive relationship because of fear, loneliness, or loss. The dreadful thought of having to start all over again or the unknown possibilities to find another mate keeps them stuck where they are. They might think, "How will this affect the kids?" and "How can I afford this upset?" I maintain that if human beings had a lower pain threshold, they would be quicker to change. After all, we are motivated by pain or pleasure. If we get enough pain in an area of our life, we are forced to change the circumstances. Pleasure can also buoy us into changing our behavior; it will feel good to move toward this action.

The key here is to incessantly check in with what you are *Feeling*. Remember you always, always, only attract into your life that which you are, not what you want. *Feeling* is the great secret to the law of attraction. In order to connect to what you want, you must feel what you want as if it is here Now. The couple in the above example is connecting to a reciprocal negative energy. They are in effect attracting each other through the feelings of distain for each other. If one has the present moment awareness of a good feeling and can awaken from the fog of habitual chilling behavior, change can take place.

Anthony Robbins (known for his motivational books and life-transforming seminars) teaches, "It is in your moments of decision that your destiny is shaped." Tony teaches people how to change. He directs people to declare "Enough!" Then, feel what you want to attract into your life. You close your eyes and you imagine the feeling of the relationship you want. You see what that looks like in your imagination. You stay with this practice of feeling in that state of being. Your new decision is now forming in you. The next time you have a confrontation with your partner, you come from a different place than before. The energy of love is greater than any power, hate, or negativity that used to have power over you. The other person will soon change to your greater power of attraction or you will separate like oil and water.

Another transformational power I have learned is the ancient Hawaiian practice of Ho'oponopono. It simply means "cleaning your energy" or point of attraction. When you choose to "clean," you offer no resistance to the other person, (using our couple as an example.) You imagine that person filled with joy or completely content in their new life. You say in your heart or out loud, *Please forgive me, I am sorry, thank you, I love you.* As you see that person in peace and love, you feel that in your body and soul. You "clean" your energy so that you will only attract like energy of that peace and contentment in your life.

Another significant error I find our fellow human beings making with regards to connection is rejecting kindness and gifts from others. Let's say you are out with a group of friends for dinner. You are about to finish this life-giving or even just simple fun gathering of food and friendship. That inherent moment comes when the check is presented by the server. Only you attract the attention of the server and motion to come to you, before the rest of the table can notice what is happening. You secretly hand the server your credit card and instruct that you are treating the table to the meal. You sign your name and place a bountiful tip out of the goodness of your heart. All of this is done under the table, so no one can see. One of the group at the table inquires, "Where is the check?" You kindly announce that you have treated everyone to the night's fun and festivities. Half of the table is grateful and appreciative. The others are adamant about paying their share of the bill. It becomes quite a commotion and some will not let it go. Eventually it becomes awkward, hence you cave in, out of sheer embarrassment in a public place.

The point of attraction for the gift giver was just disconnected. The universal law of attraction will respond in kind to the gift giver with the like energy of the gift. By taking away the collective energy of gratitude from the table, the naysayers crush the attraction. It is imperative to remember always, "Gratitude is the best multiplier." When you are thankful and share that gracious feeling with others, you just charged that energy field of attraction. In essence, you are giving a gift as well, when you receive a gift. You are responding with your gracious love and reciprocity. If more of us were connected to the feelings of *Good* (which is God), we would elevate the collective consciousness of the planet. Seemingly small instances like a dinner with friends might appear insignificant. However, we are reminded in Matthew 18:20, "For where two or three are gathered together in my name, there am I in the midst of them." Then from that *Good*, Jesus tells us how that will change our individual lives: "Give, and it will be given to you. A good measure, pressed down, shaken together and running over, will be poured into your lap. For with the measure you use, it will be measured to you" (Luke 6:38).

Your Point of Attraction

Our daily lives have a way of carrying us along this lazy river called routine. Most of us simply do not pay attention to what is showing up in response to our state of being. The numbing effect of *Doing* takes all the energy out of our *Being*. The true Art of Connection is the present moment awareness that controls your state of being. To be a Now-ist is to continually check-in with your awareness of being or the state that you are in. The beauty of present moment awareness is that you can choose to change that state instantly. The dictionary defines a *State* as, "The particular condition that someone or something is in at a specific time." By controlling your *State*, you are controlling your point of attraction. The universe will only attract that which it is like. Should you find yourself in a state contrary to your authentic self, you can change that point of attraction by changing your *State* of being.

For millions of people changing their state usually means some type of drug, drink, food, or the like. However, this choice always leads to a dead connection. There is no power in consuming false energy. They can never get enough of what they do not want. It will remain an addiction because you can never fill that hole with that energy source. The hole that remains can only be filled with the awareness of being. You cannot fool your authentic self. Your state of being is reacting to the lack of connection to your source. Emotions of stress, loneliness, fear and worry are our mind tricking us in chronological time. We are attached to a feeling that goes against who we really are. Living in a state of perceived low energy or negative energy occurs when you are focused on an ill feeling or emotion, and give it life in time. After all, *Energy flows where focus goes.*

The Now-ist presence of being lives in no time. You make a new choice about a life-situation and charge it with love and good feelings. That new choice lives in the only moment you ever have, which is here and Now. This Now-ist state of being is the powerful practice that takes you from, *Nowhere* to *NOWhere*. I realize that sometimes it just seems too difficult to break out of a negative or downward state of being. Your thinking mind is trapping you in that never-ending merry-go-round of habit. You have to jump off that ride in order to interrupt the momentum of circular habitual thinking. This jump does take a leap of faith. The old adage, "familiarity breeds comfort," usually straps us on to that shiny horse on the ride and just keeps going around and around and around. What you need is a massive push into the mysterious unknown. You must experience a jolt to your state of being in order to break out of that negative spiral. The eternal wisdom from German-born theoretical physicist Albert Einstein (1879-1955), once again encourages us to take a quantum leap: "The most beautiful thing we can experience is the mysterious. It is the true source of all Art and Science."

The Power States

Here are three methods for transforming your negative states into powerful and positive states of being. Once you create these kinds of habits, it becomes second nature to live as a Now-ist.

Physiology- The manner in which you live in your body, affects your point of attraction in the largest way. We know that energy is attracted to like energy. This is the definition of the *Law of Attraction* or the *Law of Love*. Your energy is stored in the temple of your body. We were first made aware of this fact in 1 Corinthians 6:19, "Do you not know that your bodies are temples of the Holy Spirit, who is in you, whom you have received from God?" How do you live in your body? Do you often find yourself with posture that looks like a wet towel slumped over a chair? Are your facial muscles slack with eyes low and disengaged? Do you feel shallow breathing with your shoulders forward and hunched? This can all be changed in a moment's notice by correcting your physiology. Awareness is the key to your point of attraction.

To change your physiology, you must physically move your body in a new and powerful way. When I am stuck in a poor state, my Now-ist presence instantly strikes into action. My favorite method of instant *Connection Correction* to source energy is via my "Super Hero State." *Batman* is always the image that comes to mind when daily living attempts to bring me down. I imagine the act, then respond in kind, by standing strong with my shoulders back, chest out, and my chin held high. I see the big black cape flowing behind me in the wind. My facial muscles are full of confidence and joy. I am unstoppable! This instant transformation, completely changes my posture and physical being. The next time you find yourself in a less than powerful state, choose your Super Hero and strike into action. You can save the day... and yourself!

Breathing- The breath is the life-giving action of God. Who beats our heart? Who placed the sun precisely the distance from the earth, therefore sustaining life and giving us oxygen from the plants to breathe? Do we need to think about circulating our blood? All of this and millions of other bodily functions come from the grace of God. Breathing, however, is a most powerful involuntary function of the body and can transform your life. When you take a powerful conscious breath, it anchors you in the Now. The next time that you feel stress, anxiety, fear, or impatience, stop the thinking mind by relaxing wherever you are. Allow your body to rest. Close your eyes and breathe in very slowly and deeply. The breath should start at your lower abdomen, then feel it ending at the top of your head. Three patient, slow breaths while relaxing your body will interrupt that negative pattern of attraction and clear your thinking mind. This amazingly simple action uses the body as the portal to presence. One conscious breath taken many times a day will teach you the power of connection, via the God that is you. French poet, novelist, and dramatist of the Romantic Movement,

Victor Hugo (1802-1885) made life breathless and transforming with his every deep breath creation: "Love is a portion of the soul itself, and it is of the same nature as the celestial breathing of the atmosphere of paradise."

Imagination- Imagination is the greatest gift we have ever been given. This is the ultimate transformational modality of life. When you imagine, you are a creator. You have the ability to create worlds and exist in them via your new imagined state of being. The power of this mode is to imagine with awareness from the end. In other words, see yourself with all the tones of reality in your new imagined state of being. You experience all of this reality from the end as if it has already occurred. Your imagination does not know the difference between the current time and imaginal time. Now that you know this, try it out. I want you to believe and feel the imaginal action of *Imaging in*. You image in your mind and feel it as an actualized fact in the world. This experience would go something like this.

Closing my eyes and in a relaxed body position, I see myself looking into the eyes of my soulmate. I focus on the vibrant color of her eyes. This brilliant blue I am looking into makes me feel warm and inspired. I can smell the perfume she is wearing and it is the most wonderful smell I have ever experienced. Next, I take her by the hand and we are walking together on the beach. The warm breeze from the ocean is like a hug and the sand is soft and soothing to my feet. I take out a blanket from the basket that I have been carrying and spread it out on the beach. We sit side-by-side and I hold a strawberry for her to bite. Once she takes a bite, the smell of strawberry fills the air, and the ocean breeze is now flavored with this scent. The sun is now setting into the sea, and the embrace with her, is the oneness your heart and soul has been searching for all along.

The Law of Love, or the Law of Attraction as it is also called, does not discriminate. When you consistently imagine with deep-held feelings, you will create this reality. You are thinking from the end. You are already there in your heart, body, mind, and soul. When you awake from your imaginal state of being, it should be difficult for you to separate the two states. You are completely invested in this truth. The best moments to activate the Law of Love is just before you fall asleep and right before you get out of bed in the morning. Your subconscious mind is the power station of your imagination. When you start to feel drowsy and your mind is preparing for sleep, your imagination will take that *Soulmate Scene* and replay it over and over again. It will become anchored into your being. With repetition and belief, the universe will conspire to attract these circumstances. Resulting, this imaginal act will indeed become reality. You must think from the end and not about the end. The key here is to not set some goal of having a soulmate. You are already there in your imagination. It already exists in time and space. The creator and artist that you are is the key. The Now is the key. Unlock your imagination and you are free forever. Italian polymath and a prime exemplar of a Renaissance Man, Leonardo da Vinci (1452-1519) embedded forever: "Whatever exists in the universe, whether in essence, in act, or in the imagination, the painter has first in his mind and then in his hands."

CHAPTER 4

SYNCHRONISTIC THINKING

---❖---

"Synchronicity is an ever present reality
for those who have eyes to see."

— Carl Jung

Light is the purpose of Synchronistic Thinking. The greatest dharma (purpose) one could possibly have is to be connected at all times to the oneness of all that is or ever has been. When you are in total and pure alignment with the truth of your being, who you really are shines through. The brilliant German theologian, philosopher, and mystic, Mister Eckhart (1260-1328) framed time as such: "Time is what keeps the light from reaching us. There is no greater obstacle to God than time." Human beings are challenged by the waves of information coming at each one of us daily. Our senses are being barraged endlessly. The five senses remove us from present moment states of being. Most people's attention is easily led astray with an eye-glance or unexpected events such as noises, smells, and discomfort in the physiology of one kind or another. It is one's senses that seem to be the culprit in the lack of awareness and perpetuating present moment energy suckers. Clarity of mind, body, and spirit only shines through when you have balanced the senses to a point of peaceful-awareness.

Walking down a dark street, eyes darting from side-to-side, and hearing the crash of a garbage can falling over with the smells of the sewer filling your nostrils. Fear! Our imagination fills in all the blanks, before the truth of this scene even has a chance to reveal itself. A twelve-year-old boy is shaking in the cold, the light from the moon reflects off the iced-over snow. His heart is racing. It is 3 a.m. and his brother, father, and uncle are deep asleep as he nervously stares out the camper window next to his thinly-padded bed. A sound rings out through the canyon that paralyzes the boy. If a woman screamed at the top of her lungs and a wolf howled at exactly the same time, it would barley make a comparison to this bone-rattling scare. Uncle Gil is up now making coffee on the stove. He shoots me a look that is fierce, yet concerned. Dead silence in the camper- "That was a Sasquatch!"

This was the first time I could remember all five of my senses stretched to the maximum limit in an instant. Unmitigated and utter terror! The thinking mind can take us to heaven or hell in a flash of momentum. I can remember that moment anytime I place my full attention on it. If I choose to close my eyes, picture the sites, sounds, smells, and even tastes in that moment, I am right back there in no time. Our ability to focus energy is powerful. We largely take it for granted. In order to attract into your life the manifestation you desire, you must have a complete awareness and control of the five senses. Most of us allow our senses to drag us along this current of life, never taking full ownership over how they can collectively buoy us from sinking to lower levels of undesired outcomes.

Taking back your being

If you are reading this book, chances are you have studied, meditated, attended yoga, churches, prayer services, and many other spiritually alive ventures. As your connection to the divine grows, you lose the physical need to replace any part of your worldly body with the experience you are having in that fully enlightened moment. The most powerful satori of my life I experienced in the most unlikely place imaginable. (You will read the intricacies about it in the chapter "GOLF, Go On Life's Feelings"). Once, I was hovering above the planet and I disconnected completely from the worldly feelings and mind-made forms of thought and worry. That was when I realized the modality for Synchronicity. Entering "space" was as real as if I hitched a ride on the space shuttle and asked to be dropped off on the next pass over Mount Everest. I was without a "space suit" and completely detached from materialism. Looking around up there feels vast and infinite. To see, the brilliant blue line around our home planet. To smell, nothing but clean clear air. To feel, the warmth of the sunshine all around the earth. To taste, the calm and filling sensation of inner contentment. To hear, God's one and only voice... Silence.

Remarkably real and true, I have this experience many times a day. I call it "Getting Up There" (Just trust your GUT). When I intend to manifest in this life, the five senses must be fully engaged and set to zero gravity. The light of my being shines its brightest when it is one with all of God's creation. As I hover above the earth, I feel like I am just another one of the planets in the universe. I am equal and one of creation's beloved attractors. When I completely think from the end and not about the end, pure manifestation takes place.

Here is a sound example of trusting my GUT. I tremendously wanted to sell a property that I was listing. I then channeled this brilliant quotation from the Greek novelist/essayist, Nikos Kazantzakis (1883-1957): "By believing passionately in something that still does not exist, we create it. The nonexistent is whatever we have not sufficiently desired." After months of no calls or showings and very little interest in it at all, I decided to wake up and use my GUT. I imagined from my heavenly vantage point, a family in the home. There was a blonde mother, a brown-haired father with a child and a sweet, little puppy. I could feel the love coming from the house as they smiled, laughed, and were filled by the purchase of their new dream home. I repeated this GUT feeling each morning and night for a week. On the eighth day, I received a call from an agent with a family of that very description. They wanted to see the property. It only took one showing. A day later, they made an offer and not long after my GUT reaction was actualized.

So how do we enter that "Light" state of being and attract into our lives what we most desire? Pure-present-whole-hearted-oneness with the moment is the answer of the Now-ist. Yes, it is that basic. Through the ancient teachings and spiritual masters' enlightenment, we have been made aware of this truth. Yet, most of the planet continues to live in desperation, stress, and pain. The good news is more and more sentient beings are stepping into the truth of the light. My ultimate calling is to share the love I feel deep in my soul and shine this truth as a Now-ist. Once you focus your truth in the present moment regularly, you will experience the shift in your own life and never be the same again. I find the ratio of 90/10 to be the best balance of day-in/day-out living. For instance, I spend 90 percent of my day internally focused on the present moment in whatever shape or form the Now takes. This is felt oneness with the truth and peace that is always there within us. I do not mean to make this sound simplistic or easy to maintain. I have learned that repetition is the mother of skill. My thoughts must be in alignment with oneness and present moment awareness. Oh yes, life will do its best to take you out every other minute of the day. Trust in yourself. You were made from stardust. You come from oneness. You were formed out of the universe just like one of the planets. I always tell myself these mantras:

"I am that I am the conquering presence in the Now."

"I have nothing to do, only to be done."

"I am altogether God and God is altogether me."

"I am the Light of the world."

These types of incantations keep me in the 90 percent daily. The other 10 percent of my day is driving to appointments, writing emails, and making decisions, you know, actual work tasks. This ratio of living gives momentum to your point of attraction. When you can stack moment after moment in divine awareness, synchronistic action is possible with conscious guidance.

Can you remember a time when you felt like you were really on a roll? The times when you knew you could not miss. You were totally in the flow of the moment. Your thinking mind just faded into the background. This is a truth I experience on a daily basis, and when it does, I stop and think to myself:

"I am amazed by how today's events just seem to align with perfect timing and sync." An appointment will get canceled. Then, the other commitment I had will miraculously call to see if I can meet one hour earlier, minutes after that very cancelation. Frequently, I am inspired to give or be of service in some way, not intending to be altruistic, just paying attention to the signs life is showing me. When I come from that place of service, it is like I was just awarded the key to the city. Parking spaces just magically show up in a crowded lot. People will invite you to go ahead of them in line. The check-out person will offer your daughter a free balloon just because they "feel" like it. Connections are harmoniously made that are in alignment with my present state of oneness to all that is Now. Furthermore, an event takes place in your day that seems like the universe is just giving you a wink. When I get that wink, I have learned to pay attention and open my spiritual eyes.

Simple Synchronicity

Growing up in a big Italian family with four sisters and one brother made for a multi-layered and adventurous up-bringing. My dad and mom got divorced when I was seven years old. It was a hard time growing up through the ultimate disillusion of our family and split right down the middle of my six siblings. Each of the kids had to choose in front of a judge which parent s/he wanted to live with. My older sister Wendy and younger best-buddy brother Gib chose my dad or "Pa" as I lovingly call him. Eldest sister Cindy and next-in-line Mindy, plus baby Jenny, moved in with Mom. My Pa and his three kids were invited to live with my Nana and Uncle Jack on their incredible ranch with cows, pigs, chickens, and other assorted animals. Nana was always the most powerful member of the Mandarino family. It was obvious to me that she was an angel sent from heaven like Mother Theresa.

Saint Teresa of Calcutta (1919-1997), Albanian-Indian, Roman Catholic nun and missionary, proclaimed: "I see Jesus everywhere in all of his disguises." Unquestionably, Nana was and will always be a saint in my heart. She could straighten you right up with a simple step into her kitchen. She made the most incredible bread you ever tasted! She called it the "staff of life." Her bread was the symbol of her love. Just like the story in the bible of Jesus feeding the multitudes with fish and loaves, Nana's bread came from the same love of abundance and selfless affection. Not only did she make mouth-watering bread, everything she created tasted and felt like Christmas morning in your heart. The kind of attention she uniquely commanded came with a warm presence and fierce, yet peaceful, countenance. She would give you her famous "shirt-chest treatment," if you needed an awakening to what was really going on in the moment. I can still feel her grab me by the shirt and lovingly twist it up in her fist, as she conveyed her hypnotic truth right into your eyes. My Nana had the best one-liners and the simplest way of looking at life.

She let whatever inspired her in the moment to come flying out of her head and right through her perfectly, cavity-free, mouth. Just one of

Nana's incredible feats of purity in her 93 years on earth! A most famous and frequent saying of hers was "ignorance is bliss." In this day and age, ignorance is looked down upon and considered a lowly state of being. However, my grandmother in her eminent wisdom always came to the conversation with piercing truth and deliberate intention. To me, simplicity in thought with no clutter in mind, is the ignorance (is bliss) she speaks of. This quote and teaching rings in my memory from our beloved Nana. The bliss she confidently portrayed in her life is likened to the teacher leading by example, never having to explain herself or her poetic, inspirational words. Once she locked on to you and you were caught in her powerful stare, you knew something of deep-rooted truth was about to be revealed. She then reiterated it to ensure that you got the message and lesson in one fell swoop.

The simple focus of mind and blissful peace Nana spoke of was always ahead of its time. I did not know it as a boy, even though I had a deep inner reception for her certainty and respectful ways. This commonly used phrase, "ignorance is bliss" would ultimately become the basic theme of this book. The truth is spoken in many simple ways. We usually let it slip right past us like a familiar friend whom we just cannot remember their name. Yet, time and time again, it is right there sitting in our ears and waiting for us to grab hold of it.

Psalm 46:10 teaches and assures, "Be still and know I Am God." The first time I read this as a teenager, I did not understand the truth. I casually read the bible at age 13 cover-to-cover, yet the enormity and specificity of the content glazed me over. I remembered this passage however. It seemed simple, all-encompassing and profound. Now emerging into my 50s, and the world has sunk its teeth in me, I know the truth about this passage. I have found it to be the consummate parallel to our wise-family, matriarch's advice.

"Be still..." Become one with the now. To be still is the connection to the timeless present moment. Life is always just now. There is no time when your life was not Now. Everything that has ever happened to you, happened in a present moment of one sort or another. The stillness is the space between all time. That is the great hidden secret to timelessness. We search for time in everything we do. Begging for our life's situation to measure up with the thought that lives in time and has its being in a time-bound event. This is the illusion and most seductive mind-suck that we allow ourselves to succumb.

"and Know..." Here it is. "Know" and be careful with the thinking mind! Your cognitive mind can overrule your now existence. This passage "Be still and know I am God" from the great scriptures should be referenced as frequently as the Corinthians' passage, "love is patient and love is kind." We spend too much time with useless thinking, then ruminating on what to do. The fear and indecision in the thinking let us down the moment we surrender to it. The life we want to live resides in the spacious awareness from the thinking. We stay too close to the thought. Our attention and energy is wasted on this modality of the judgmental mind. I maintain the truth is found in the unknown. The ultimate expansion of our hearts and minds is in the realm of no thought. The bliss we feel and more importantly create with the awareness of being "still" lifts us up and out of the pit of the limited thought forms the "knowing" mind numbingly drags us down.

Nana left this world with the same honesty and truth she lovingly imprinted on the hearts she touched. Her final words to me were, "We sure had some fun, didn't we Billy Boy." I will never forget the simple joy in her brown eyes and the presence of fearless love emanating from her being. I was made aware of the eternal present Now in that hospital room. She had no regrets and only wisdom of the heart's truth to share with those she left behind....

"The Ring Masters"

My brother Gib and I had always dreamed of going to the Masters golf tournament in Augusta, Georgia. This is the biggest golf event on the true golf fan's calendar. Year after year, we would talk on the phone after the first few rounds, and of course after the eventual winner garnered the cherished Green Jacket on championship Sunday. One day, I called my bro up and pitched, "Hey, do you want to go to the Masters?" It gave me as much excitement as my brother to even hear those words uttered. This is like going to Mecca for golfers. After jubilant cheers celebrating on the phone and months of planning, we were on our way. The trip from my home in Santa Barbara, California was literally all the way across the country. Once we arrived at that little airport, you knew golf was in the air.

Augusta National Golf Club was truly, jaw-dropping, gorgeous. Walking the hallowed fairways and watching the Georgia pines sway in the breeze was a sort of religious experience. We had the best brother-bonding time imaginable.

This trip was one of the most powerfully synchronistic events I have ever had. You see, my brother was at a crossroads in his life. Though blessed with a beautiful family of three daughters, after being together for more than twenty years, the feelings and passion left the marriage. My brother is the most dedicated father you could ever meet. Most of his days are spent working and caring for his beloved girls. He and I had many hours-long conversations about his choices and options for his marriage. The fact that I could afford to take us on this trip and his need for clarity were purely heaven-sent. (Truly, Synchronistic abundant Thinking has been very good to me!) I asked him, while at the Masters, if he could imagine a setting to take his mind off the worry and indecision, where would he go? He did not even have to answer my question. He paused, open his arms, and gestured, here and Now.

The two of us lived each step as if it were our last, focused and breathing in the action of the most famous golf tournament in the world. We experienced two full days of action and spectacular golf. Each night as we walked back to the hotel, we would share and work through his feelings, trying to create the space for his family's ultimate happiness and well-being. Reminding my brother how powerful his point of attraction is, "Energy flows where your focus goes," I chanted. Encouraging him to place his attention, his power of intention, on what he wants to manifest and create, I spoke of thoughts being things (to come) and thinking from the end, not about the end. We were both blessed to be in such a healing state of awareness, singularly present at this awe-inspiring event, allowing us to vamp about both our marital experiences to find the truth and essence of what was best for his family.

On the last morning of the trip we headed to the airport, the sweetest little airport you could imagine for a golfer. A statue of Bobby Jones greeted you in the center of the main terminal. The Rolex clock towered over the busy travelers. Everyone was pleasant and engaging. As Gib and I approached the ticketing desk to collect our boarding passes, we were met by a kind woman wearing glasses with colorful frames. She was naturally bubbly and exuberant.

"You're going to Santa Barbara!" She boldly announced.

Before we could explain the trip and the wonderful details, she was off on her own run down memory lane, "I was born in Santa Barbara and raised in Santa Barbara. I love the beaches there. I left it in 1987 to move here."

On and on, it went until she shot out her right hand and said, "Look! I even have my class ring. I never take it off!"

I could tell she was eager for me to see it, took it off, and handed it to me.

"It feels so weird not to have it on my finger," she immediately interjected.

Looking at it closely, I could see the words *San Marcos High School* inscribed on it.

I instantly proclaimed, "My wife is a teacher there!"

This did not phase the woman, yet, it shocked me. I texted a picture of it to my wife. The woman continued to ramble on about Santa Barbara neighborhoods that she lived in and places she loved to eat. Generally, she just had a crazy look in her eyes.

Handing her back the ring, she moaned about how good it felt to have it on her finger. Meanwhile, she was checking us in during this entire exciting exchange. She gave us our boarding passes. We shared a few more reminiscent moments of life in Santa Barbara as we headed off to our gate. I walked about 10 steps and realized that I was missing my suitcase. Oh no! I checked it onto the plane! (Prior to the trip, Gib and I had vowed to not check any bags since we had to take four planes to Santa Barbara). My wedding ring was in my shaving kit! Because I had lost bags on airlines before, my thoughts instantly went to a negative place. Worry took me away. In the moment, speaking of rings, my brother told me that his wedding ring had fallen off his finger at a friend's house recently. Though he found it, he felt it was a sign of events to come.

Then the most amazing thing happened to me. In a flash, a mental movie ran through my awareness. It went something like this: The crazy lady that checked us in was so excited about Santa Barbara, my hometown, that she inadvertently checked in my bag. Synchronistically, she had her high school class ring which was from my wife's school. I felt like I lost my ring because she distracted me to the degree that the momentum of the conversation made me check in my bag. I expressed to my brother fear, worry, and doubt out of reflex to the situation.

Surely, this was all happening for a reason. The ring she showed me was a symbol that my ring was safe. Hence, I imagined that after traversing the country on four different planes, my wedding ring would be there in Santa Barbara at the luggage pick up. Once I had this realization, I knew that it was a transformational moment to show synchronistic faith in action! I recounted the whole story that rushed into my mind with my brother as we sat on the plane waiting for take off. Just as I finished my story, the crazy gate lady burst onto the plane and yelled, "I hope you all enjoyed the Masters!" Gib and I looked at each other and exclaimed, "What the heck was that?" I have never had a gate attendant do that before, especially when the counter was that far away from the plane. We both laughed and acted like stun-gun victims.

We attempted to rationalize what had just happened. Before we got too far down that train of thought, it hit us. This was a confirmation sign. In her crazy passionate state of mind, she gave us a great gift. The ultimate exclamation punctuation to the synchronistic event I just shared with my bro. This all happened for him, not me. I further elaborated. The universe gives us what we need, exactly when we need it. I whole-heartedly embrace this Marcus Aurelius (121-180) wisdom: "Accept whatever comes to you woven in the pattern of your destiny, for what could more aptly fit your needs."

When we open our minds and hearts to what is, and why it is there for us, we find ourselves to be in a new world. The average day of the most average person on the planet is full of synchronistic events. They just do not have the awareness of being to place themselves in the picture of divine order and circumstance. Imagine if this kind of *Synchronistic Thinking* occurred on a daily basis for the planet. If a meager 3.14 percent of the earth's population had the daily practice of *Synchronistic Thinking*, then they would manifest what they want. We would create "Phase Transition" or "The Hundredth Monkey Effect" known in the scientific academia. Of course, the intention of the being has to come from a good place to attract into your life your most sought after desires and wishes. This is the summation of what I feel and believe to be the best kept secret to manifestation. This mystery is encoded in our daily lives' comings and goings, just underneath your nose, yet vaporizing like a mist in the jungle. Once you deeply understand this next rung on the ladder of higher awareness, you will see from atop this perfect pinnacle. The ancient Persian-Muslim, poet and theologian, Rumi (1207-1273) exalts us still: "The day you were born, a ladder was set up to help you escape the world." Absolutely, we need to be conscious of what life is showing us in order to direct our intentions to the highest good.

Chapter 5

The Conscious Conductor

--- ⯆ ---

"Music is the purest form of art… therefore true
poets, they who are seers, seek to express the
universe in terms of music. The singer has everything
within him. The notes come out from his very life.
They are not materials gathered from outside."

— Rabindranath Tagore

One of the most brilliant artists of all time, in my opinion, was Prince. This genius won numerous awards in countless artistic arenas. The volumes of music that he created is vast enough that an album could be released each year for the next 100 years! His artistic interpretation spans more musical genres than almost any other artist in the world. Prince's connection to spirit, source energy, and God was direct and intensely honest. To witness this brilliant musician perform and interpret his art live was a manifestation of the soul's existence. He would make a believer out of each and every audience member. His truth was always left on the stage, for all to hear, see, and most importantly feel.

It has been said that people either loved Prince or hated him. He did not mince his art or water it down for the masses. He spoke soulfully and connected to his honesty. Some shunned his music in fear of the unknown because society wants the hero to fit into a box of commonality and conformity. The great ones, however, carve their own path and take the road less traveled. Our pillars and role models of the impossible cut through the vail of existence with no apologies or regret. They are the examples to follow, yet they teach us to go our own way. More times than not, we need to find where the masses go and choose the other direction.

Prince departed this earth a better place than when he entered it. His contribution will live on forever. He inspired with the greatest of ease. One of the most incredible events happened when he made his transition to the non-physical realm of spirit. In my recollection, only Prince and Dr. Wayne Dyer have ever made their transition to the heavenly plane with such profundity. Prince was ill and battled a couple of different maladies. He was on what would become his last journey of shows, *The Piano and Microphone Tour*. This was such a fitting format, and title, for his climactic tour given the fact that playing and writing music on the piano was how he started his musical career. His first instrument of nearly forty instruments was the piano. In addition, he wrote his very first song on a piano.

This phenom of an artist always did things the way of his inspiration and never followed the crowd. *Of course*, he signed-off from this life to the afterworld in his perfectly Prince manner. You see, this genius was very private and to himself. Residing in his Paisley Park Studios apartment on the back half of his property, he was alone and found in his elevator unconscious. He ascended to the heavenly realm inside that elevator. I am sure he knew exactly what he was doing in true Prince form. Here is where the story gets amazing!

The only hit song Prince ever wrote that began with a church organ and theme of a sermon to the congregation was "Let's Go Crazy." He preaches:

> …instead of asking him how much of your time is left, ask him how much of your mind, baby, cause in this life, things are much harder than in the afterworld. In this life, you're on your own. *And if the elevator tries to bring you down, go crazy, punch a higher floor.*

In an interview with Chris Rock for VH1 in 2012, Prince explains the meaning of his elevator metaphor in "Let's Go Crazy." The elevator dropping is meant to represent the devil, while *punching a higher floor* means getting closer to God. Prince was a devout, God-fairing man. He was entirely aware of his I AM presence. He was altogether God and God was altogether him.

I am sure he entered the elevator that night fully aware and present that it was his time to go. More importantly, where he was going. In his ultimate artistic finale, he finished the song and his life with these prophetic words: **"Take me away!"**

Dr. Wayne W. Dyer had an equally powerful end to his new beginning. This incredible spiritual teacher wrote forty books and appeared on countless television and radio shows. Millions of people have been inspired and moved to higher awareness because of this being, one that I have loved seeing and reading his works. Despite the first ten years of his life in and out of foster homes and hating a father that he never even met, he manifested his first quantum moment when he was thirty-four years old as a teacher at St. John's University in New York. That day following an incredible journey of synchronicity, Dr. Wayne found himself at his father's grave site. Once there, he was overwhelmed with rage to a level that incited him to urinate on this disgraceful man's grave. Sobbing and hysterical, he would later explain that something came over him. He walked away from the site and minutes later returned. This time in an act of profound forgiveness he states, "From this moment on, I send you love." Remarkably, Dr. Wayne never lost belief in himself and forgiveness though he had feelings of hate and dreams of beating up his phantom father. The date, August 30th, 1974, would become the most important act of forgiveness of his entire life. After this prophetic encounter, Dr. Wayne drove to Florida and checked into a hotel. There, he wrote his first book in just fourteen days. *Your Erroneous Zones* would go on to sell over 55 million copies and change the lives of countless souls!

This was just his first book, mind you. He had a ritual that would open his connection to the divine. At 4:14 a.m. every morning, he awoke and wrote in the silent peace; that was his way. This brilliant writer would later be known as the "Father of Motivation." He never liked that moniker. As the father of eight children, he did not "need" to be the father of anything else, he stated. However, he could embrace being the "Father of Inspiration" because the concept and teaching of inspiration (vs. motivation) became his ultimate calling.

Later in life, Dr. Wayne contracted leukemia. He opted to follow the synchronistic signs and people that presented themselves in his life for treatment. He shunned the western forms of radiation, surgery, and chemotherapy. The main healing event in his life was done via "Remote

Entity Healing" through a healer named John of God. Dr. Wayne experienced a healing that would change his life forever and explains it fully in his incredible book *Wishes Fulfilled*. As a "Conscious Conductor" this giant of a soul was tapped in, tuned in and turned on to his divine connection always. His purpose, or dharma as it is called in the east, was crystal clear for him, "Teach others self reliance." He opened up a portal via his awareness and shared it with the world. Inspiration and love were his dharma, while his sagacious voice always shined the wisdom through.

August 30th, 2015 at 4:14 a.m., Wayne W. Dyer returned to spirit, in being, entirely. This was the day forty years earlier that he changed the world with his one act of forgiveness. He wrote his books connected to divine inspiration at 4:14 a.m. Later, the autopsy would report that no cancer was in his body whatsoever! Additionally, his heart just stopped beating to this worldly rhythm. When his family floated his ashes out to sea in Maui, where he loved to swim each day, one of his daughters took a picture with her iPhone. As the sun was setting, you can clearly see his face in the ocean ripples on the surface. There are no coincidences. All is divine order and perfect synchronicity. Dr. Wayne's famous quotation encourages us all to heed his advice: "When you change the way you look at things, the things you look at change."

I choose Prince and Dr. Wayne as the two power houses of spirit and inspiration because they have and continue to change the world with divine connection. They did not die with their music still inside them. Truth of heart and soul was revealed for all to see and most importantly feel. They always consciously connected to the divine and allowed spirit to flow through them and into the world, via their art. When you free yourself from the world and enter that space of pure presence, you are one with the divine inspiration that intended you here, Now. To be a *conscious conductor* is to live in that Now-ist presence. Countless gifted souls have shined that light and inspired the world with their art, connected in pure presence.

To share the light is the enlightened being's call. It is only natural to be like that from which you came. We all came from the non-physical and we will all return to it. The key here is to realize that we all have a special gift from God. How could a universe that works perfectly in sync with the surrounding elements be a "Big Bang" of accidents? Imagine a huge explosion blew up an entire printing factory. While cleaning up, a worker discovers on the ground a perfectly clean and unharmed dictionary with thousands of words and detailed pages, a book seamless in design and form. Yet this is created by a random explosion via an "accident?"

When you consciously conduct your life, all becomes simple and clear. The intelligence that creates worlds is the same power you have within you. If you were to take a bucket of ocean and put it right in front of you, then look back at the ocean from the beach where you stand, that bucket of ocean is altogether the ocean and the ocean is altogether in the bucket. It is only when you separate that ocean from its source of origin that it eventually evaporates into thin air. The great awareness is to realize that oneness with your source. You came from an energy source that is altogether God and God is altogether you. To live each day in Now-ist awareness is to connect again and again to that realization.

The Music of the Soul

I remember the first time I ever saw the symphony. Our junior high class went to the opera house for a field trip. Choir and band were very important to me. As the auditorium of over two thousand students settled down, a brief silence came over the audience in anticipation of what we were all about to experience. The conductor stepped to the podium, looked at the musicians in front of him, and slowly raised his baton. I was riveted by the power that one person had to control the seventy plus musicians. He was running the show. Yes, of course it takes all the individual extremely talented musicians to play their part, but the power was in the conductor's hands. He led us on a dynamic musical and ethereal journey. I was deeply moved a few times during the concert; I actually had tears in my eyes and a lump in my throat. The emotion and sensation of the music lifted me in a way that I could not imagine before this day.

From that day on, music chose me. I did not choose music. Connection comes unexpectedly and abrupt; you can miss it if you are not aware. The signs are all around us. They point and guide the traveler to the next turn in the journey. My heart changed that day. I felt it in my body and spirit. My musical inspiration energetically ramped up. I began to shun the classical training of voice and instrument that I was taking. My inspiration was Now to create my own music. My father had a beautiful Ovation guitar that had been in the family for decades. It was well taken care of and not an instrument to be disrespected. When I first picked it up years before, a course of inspiration waved through me, I remembered. In awe of its beauty and craftsmanship, it just seemed anything was possible when I looked at that guitar. This was just a lovely six string static instrument. Yet, millions can be moved via the universal connection of music and spirit, if it is played with heart and soul.

We are all instruments of expression and connection. Our music is being played and broadcast all the time. If you allow sour notes and poor form to come out of you, that is what the world hears. The universal harmony or disharmony of music is all around each and every one of us. When you are tuned to a frequency of thought and emotion, you feel it in your body. The feeling then emanates from your being to the vibrational world of invisible wave forms. You will align with that feeling and bring in like waves of congruent energy. It is just like a tuning fork. When each of the instrument's strings are tuned to the proper notes individually, then a chord can be played and ring out for all to hear its beauty. It is only when we consciously conduct our own music that we experience oneness with the universal source.

The Bible refers to this experience as *The Law of Identical Harvest* or reaping what you sow. It is also popular to refer to this as The Law of Attraction. Like attracts like and it is a universal law. People in general do not make the connection between what they do, think, say, or feel and what their life is producing. Unconscious direction of your life is like a ship without a rudder to steer you and navigate the oceans of the world. I know tons of people that wish for life to send them a healing, money, a relationship, or abundance of some kind, yet never consciously connecting the power they have to attract it.

When I find that the signs of life show up in a manner that does not serve my highest callings, I pay attention. It can be emotional, physical, social, financial, or even spiritual. My threshold for pain is usual great, so it can take a little while for me to become aware of what I am attracting. Finally when I awaken, every time the solution is the same. Just be of service and give your heart and love to another. My manifesto is "You Got to Give to Live!" Jesus tells us how to deal with scarcity in our lives. He instructs in Luke 6:38, "Give, and it will be given to you. A good measure, pressed down, shaken together and running over, will be poured into your lap. For with the measure you use, it will be measured to you."

This is the universal law that governs abundance and will take you out of whatever you are resisting. Here are two great reminder quotations, "What you resist persists," and "Energy flows where your focus goes." If you can just speed up your awareness, that is the key to becoming a Nowist. You must consciously connect what you are attracting into your life with your desires. Your peace and presence is the key to your point of attraction. When you are angry, sad, wronged, or even lost, the solution is the same. Here is a step-by-step process to take you out of scarcity and into abundance.

1. Start by taking the focus off yourself.
2. Find someone or some place that is in need.
3. Make your new intention to be of service in whatever way inspires you in that moment of giving.
4. Give consistently until you have the awakening to the Law of Identical Harvest.

Here are some examples of what this might look like in the world and in transformation to transmute base metal into gold through alchemy. This is your personal power. Once you begin to live your life as a pure *conscious conductor*, your life will never be the same.

Sad, lonely or discouraged: Find the signs that are showing up in your life. A person might continue to cross your path that is even worse off than you feel you are. Reach out and give to them. Find that elderly person who has no hope or does not feel needed any longer. Go to them and just talk and visit, never discussing your malady or the like. Connect with a little child. Learn from their simplicity and joy by just being in the moment as they are. Let go of your ego. My favorite acronym, EGO, from Dr. Wayne Dyer for *ego* is Edging God Out. We edge God out with our self-centered pride. By taking the attention off yourself and giving to others, you will squash that ego and attract what you are, not just what you want.

Financial scarcities: The key here is to change the way you look at financial abundance. If you look at your bank account and see a scary number, you just activated that feeling in your body and the spirit of scarcity. Imagine the three ghosts from Dickens' classic story, *A Christmas Carol* (1843). Only, replace the ghosts with this context. The ghost of the **past** is taking you on that floating journey, flying back over the worries and fears of financial scarcity. You see the times you have made bad decisions and hoarded your money with fear as your main driving force. Then, you are whisked away like a bird, ghost two, traveling to the **future** where you see your financial numbers only getting worse and worse. The fear has taken you over to such a degree that you are almost homeless and broke. Next, the ghost of the **present** lifts you above your house and you see all the bills, worries, doubts, and lack you are currently living.

Enter the fourth ghost. This is the **Now-ist** ghost. This entity has you stay right where you are. It tells you to close your eyes and imagine you are hovering above the earth. It asks you to describe the blue line around the planet. It wants to know what the stars look like up there. The ghost knows you see the ocean and the land forms below you. This spirit then asks you in the moment what it looks like and most importantly feels like to have financial abundance. You see yourself from above the earth looking down from space at the spectacular wealthy you. The heavenly spirit has you think from the end and not about the end. You are already here, now, feeling the peace come over you. You no longer have the money worries and fears that have ruled your life up to this Now-ist moment. You see yourself financially secure and abundant. That new number in your bank account is lofty; you feel in your body the joy and gratitude of your financial state.

When you open your eyes, you have a difficult time separating what you just imagined with what currently is your bank balance. The next step is to share some of what you have with those less fortunate than you. Go to a homeless person and give them some socks, food from your pantry, or whatever you feel inspired to give. Find a perfect stranger walking down the street and give them some of your cash. Bake something and deliver it to a family or a person in need. My Nana was the most amazing woman. She raised seven kids. (Grandpa Neno passed away too soon). One day she told me the story of hard times when all her children were young. Work was scarce for Grandpa and they barely had enough food to feed the family. Nana had baked three loaves of bread. Grandpa then said, "I want to take one of the loaves to our neighbor." Nana replied, "We can't afford to do that!" Then my grandfather said, "How can we afford not to?"

Social scarcity: The truth about this lack in one's life seems too simple. They are alone and detached from the community they are living in or surrounded by. This can be a selfish energy-sucking state in a life. You hoard the gift that you are to the community. We all have purpose or dharma as it is called in the east. To extract yourself from the lowly mind-set of "me," you must open your heart to "we." Find a local soup kitchen that feeds the homeless in your community. Volunteer your time and be of service to others in need. The lives you will touch will change your life in ways you could never imagine before. Another option is to volunteer at a fun run for children or adults. You will connect with like-minded individuals that want to give back. When you give to the social world what you want in your life, you will attract it in return.

Physical scarcity: "Dis-ease" or disease as it is referred to, is just that. Stress, tension, worry, fear, and negativity in the physiology. Many times in my life, illness will attempt to assail my body. The news will broadcast that the cold and flu season is upon us; be sure to run out and get your shots and medicines. They almost make it sound like it is a wave of germs and little alien beings are attacking our city. I use to have a pattern of getting a cold or flu bug every winter when the seasons changed. I had a cough for a couple months every year buying into the fear and worry of the city, setting myself up to get sick. I was offering up no positive energy to the assault on my body. The inertia of the bad news stories combined with the change of seasons set up my self talk to think in sickly and defeatist ways. Now, armed with the power of the Now-ist consciousness, I rarely ever get sick. When that feeling of illness attempts to take me over, my powerful presence focuses on my well- being and unstoppable imagination.

Yes, I do wash my hands more frequently and eat more healthy foods during this "season." However, this illness will come over my body like a cold, wet blanket. When I start to feel the first signs of this, I instantly change my focus and become filled with "ease" to replace the "dis-ease." More to the point, I close my eyes, breathe deeply and connect to my spirit. I imagine being above the planet and seeing my "lower-self" standing where ever I am at the moment. I see myself feeling in perfect health with vibrant energy and loving my vitality. I do this repeatedly until I physically feel my body here, NOW, connected to that abundance. When I am one in that moment, I descend from the heavenly realm above the earth and connect to the earthly me.

When a Now-ist is all that you are, your immunity is greatly strengthened and illness will rarely even touch you. It is like you have a force field all around you. Your point of attraction is connected to only the good, blissful states and events of life. You manifest health, wealth, joy and abundance as a natural action of being.

Your life will be an example of peace and attract like energies to you, via this law of love.

Spiritual scarcity: The overly thinking mind creates the illusion that there is a shortage of spirituality. The French mathematician and scientist, Descartes' (1596-1650) statement, "I think, therefore I am" is perhaps one of the most erroneous statements ever uttered about spirituality. He associated thinking with being, and being with thinking. Yet, thinking simply occurs, like your heart beats, and your hair grows. I AM is the name of God. It is the overly thinking mind that is the greatest obstacle to the spiritual oneness that you really are. The ancient spiritualist and founder of Siddha Yoga, Muktananda (1908-1982) stated, "That is real, which never changes." Our bodies change constantly, hence they are not real. Our being-ness never changes. The I AM presence that you are, never changes.

Here are the two simplest ways to directly connect to your spirit. Sit in a chair and relax in the moment. Allow your arms and shoulders to rest on your thighs with your hands facing palm down. Make certain you are sitting up with the spine erect and your feet are on the floor. Then close your eyes and relax your face. Take a deep breath in through your nose and fill your lungs. If you can breathe from your diaphragm that is best. Slowly release the breath out your mouth. Imagine that you are taking in light with your breath and expelling light out your breath. Three conscious breaths will connect you to the spirit and aid you in entering the Now-ist state of being.

Another great connector to the spirit that you are is through nature. It might seem too simplistic or basic to the thinking mind. However, the thinking mind is usually the main problem with this scarcity. The American naturalist John Muir (1838-1914) spoke these fine words of encouragement for connection via nature to your spirit, "The clearest way into the universe is through a forest wilderness.... The mountains are calling and I must go." Go on a hike or a walk deep into the wilderness or park. Just allow your five senses to explore and expand. Be like a child in bewilderment and awe. Imagine how infinite the worlds are all around you as you walk. There is an ant world, a plant world, a bird world, a deer world, a fox world, and a tree world. When the sun has set and you look up at the stars, like the pin holes in the curtain of night, you will feel that vast infinity you are a part of. Once you have connected to that feeling, you have consciously conducted your life.

CHAPTER 6

SIGNS IN NO TIME

"The lord whose is the oracle at Delphi neither utters
nor hides his meaning, but shows it by a sign."

— Heraclitus

Do you see Monarch butterflies? In recent experience, these angelic creatures consistently reveal themselves to me in the most amazing ways. My awareness was brought to them via an incredible story I read. Dr. Wayne Dyer recounts his prophetic introduction to these mystical beings at the end of one of his inspiring books. His dear friend Jack was a huge fan of Monarch butterflies. He just loved how they had such a short life, yet lived with great presence and purpose. These uplifting little ones traveled thousands of miles back to the same branch they were hatched to lay their eggs. They do all of this with a brain the size of a pinhead. When Dr. Wayne's buddy passed away, Jack's wife gave Wayne a Monarch butterfly paper weight to remember his beloved friend.

Years later, Dr. Wayne was on the beach in Maui contemplating his book that was almost complete. He was filled with gratitude and said out-loud, "Thank you, Thank you, Thank you." These were the words Jack would say at the end of each of his sermons when he was alive. His ministry in Detroit and his stories of the miraculous journeys of the Monarch, with gratitude being the key to connecting with God, inspired Dr. Wayne. As Dr. Wayne sat there on the beach, a Monarch butterfly landed next to him. He thought to himself how synchronistic it was for this Monarch to land right next to him as he said these now famous words of his departed friend. "Thank you, Thank you, Thank you." What happened next is a sure *sign* of the divine. The Monarch flew from being next to him to land right on his finger! If you know Monarch butterflies, they are characteristically autonomous, shy creatures. This was truly out of the ordinary. Dr. Wayne was overwhelmed; he called his editor and best friend to gush about this miracle. He was instructed by his editor to get a camera and take a picture of this Monarch on his finger. They had been struggling with what would be the book's cover photo. This was it! The butterfly did not move from his finger for over two hours! He walked one mile back to his home, and even through beach winds, the little critter clung to Wayne.

Once back at his beach house, the Monarch was placed on the handwritten Chapter 17 of the book that was almost complete. He proceeded to take a long, hot shower. When he returned, the butterfly was still there! Yet, he seemed different. Back to his autonomous ways, the inspiring little angel flapped his wings twice and off to the heavens he returned. The next morning for some reason, Wayne decided to watch one of his favorite films, *Brother Son, Sister Moon*, which he had not seen for more than a decade. And sure enough- in the opening scene of the life of St. Francis, there he was, with a butterfly alighting on his fingers!

When I read that story in the final pages of Dr. Wayne's book, *Inspiration: Your Ultimate Calling*, it changed me. My level of belief in synchronicity and signs leveled up. It was like someone took the dimmer switch attached to my feelings about the subject and lifted it to maximum power! My beloved teacher and inspirer flew away to heaven just like the Monarch butterfly on August 30th, 2015. Since Dr. Wayne's transition to pure spirit, he has been showing himself to me just like his buddy "Jack." Once, I was golfing and preparing to tee off. My thoughts were focused on ideas for this book. As I stood over the golf ball ready to swing, a Monarch butterfly grazed my hand, hovered as if to look at me, then flew away. Another time, I was driving in my car and my thoughts were inspired once again about experiences for this very chapter. As I slowed the car down to enter a driveway, a Monarch butterfly flew right into my windshield. It was not harmed. I could clearly see its wings splayed out. These types of "Synchronistic Monarch butterfly" events continually occur in my life. Yet, another experience related directly with Dr. Wayne and a Monarch butterfly happened one winter day when I was getting out of my car. At the exact moment that my heart was filled by Dr. Wayne's audio book that I had been listening to about divine love, I was literally struck between the eyes by a Monarch butterfly! I needed no further convincing of the power of signs and synchronicity in my life after that one.

How have you been impacted by signs in your own life? I am certain you could ask just about anyone and they would regale you with similar stories of the unexplained sign. Why do mountains of people experience these miraculous events, yet blow them off as a strange happenstance? The power of your awareness is there to guide you, if you pay attention, are astonished, and tell other people. My life has always been deeply connected to the unknown. I feel that that is where the true growth is. Our souls just want to expand and experience life. We cannot fence them in if we genuinely want to find joy. I believe that signs are *Spiritual Bread Crumbs*. You must follow them to find your way to the pot of gold at the end of the rainbow. You must pay attention to where they lead you. When we are in prayer, we connect to the divine realm in intention and desire. That prayer is answered when we pay attention to the intuition and inspiration we feel about the given prayer. Yes, it can take form in physical manifestation or idea. Yet, the power of your awareness is the key to the prayer's answer. More to the point, the sign that is right in front of you can lead you to revelation, direction, or the like.

Biblical and natural signs are abundant. According to the biblical story, a dove was released by Noah after the flood in order to find land; it came back carrying a freshly plucked olive leaf, a sign of life after the flood and of God's bringing Noah, his family, and the animals to land. In Christianity, a dove also symbolizes the Holy Spirit, in reference to Matthew 3:16 and Luke 3:22 where the Holy Spirit is compared to a dove at the Baptism of Jesus. This is one of the earliest signs in the bible. Another wonderful sign that gives hope for all time is the rainbow that came after the great flood. God placed a rainbow in the sky, as a covenant with Noah, that He would never flood the earth again.

The day after I wrote this rainbow passage, a huge double rainbow appeared over my daughter's school when I picked her up. Santa Barbara had been in a five year drought. That was the biggest storm the city had seen in years. Indeed! That was a pure sign of this chapter's inspiration and divine confirmation. Signs have such great power if you are present and aware. It is most important to pay attention to what you are thinking and feeling when a sign is presented. Life has a way of pulling you out of the present moment and distracting you. This is why being a Now-ist is imperative to your ultimate joy and connection to the divine that is you. When you can be busy in your day, then notice that sign that relates directly to the thought or feeling you are having that is the awareness of the Now-ist. It will lead you on the path to connected love.

The Vehicles of God

Signs can appear in the most ordinary method or modality. For years, I have used the license plate on the car I owned at the given time to foreshadow or shine light on my life. It just came over me one day to look for the hidden message in my license plate. I was deeply in love with my girlfriend (now wife) at the time. I drove four and a half hours each way every month to see her. The drive from Santa Cruz to Santa Barbara was the freeway to my love. My license plate for that car was 2PCL212. I reference the number 2 as my Love and me. The "P" stood for Platinum, the most precious metal. Then "C" represented the Chariot, the vehicle that transported royalty or the God-like. Finally, "L" was for Love. Thus, the license plate read to me as "The Platinum Chariot of Love." This is the vehicle that would transport me back and forth to my soul-mate.

My wife and I had been married for eleven years. We finally were going to have a baby. I was beyond excited and inspired that I decided to leave my current job after a decade-plus of working there in order to become a realtor. I had a vision that this profession would give me the flexible schedule I needed to be close to a stay-at-home dad. I did everything that society said was a "no no" to do at the same time. I quit my job, started a new job, sold a house, bought a house, remodeled the new house, had a baby, and bought a new car. The license plate on this new car was 3RLT321. The number 3 represents baby, wifey, and me. The abbreviation for realtor in the real estate world is RLT. The numbers 3, 2, 1, I interpret the number 3 as 3 members in my family turning into 1 divine presence, *One-Now-Won*. Since I have adopted this license plate *sign* modality, it seems as though life follows the spirit of the letters and numbers on the vehicle. This all happens during the time I own the vehicle. The universe is organizing to serve us. We just need to look for alignment, signs, and meaning that show themselves to us if we are present. I saw the confirmation in "RLT" of the license plate as a genuine sign of direction. I knew that I had made the right choice and this vehicle would carry me to a successful real estate career for my family.

The license plate on my car when I had the epiphany about being a Now-ist was 7DXH703. I decided to get an all white car. The exterior and interior were entirely white. This conscious choice I made was to purify the attraction of my life. I wanted to be focused on divine heavenly love. Keep in mind when these license plates show up in the mail for the new car, they are completely random and I do not create them, or do I? To me, the number 7 has always represented "heaven." The first number on the plate was 7. The "D" stands for Dreams. The "X" represents experience. And "H" is the first letter in the word Heaven. My inspiration from this license plate came to me the moment I opened it in the mail: "Dreams Experience Heaven." My complete feeling while reading the plate: 7-Heaven, D-Dreams, X-Experience, H-Heaven, then 7, the 0 symbolized the infinite circle of the Now and the 3 is my wife, daughter, and me.

With each vehicle I get, the license plate has a meaning which I am inspired to interpret for my own life. The 7DXH703 plate has fulfilled its message to me. When I first felt the inspiration in the message, I did not know what to expect. I did know that I would be guided and that filled me with peace. Now that I understand the meaning, I realize that it was there all along the journey. This book is the "Dream Experiencing Heaven." My success in real estate is the dream experiencing heaven. Most importantly, the Now-ist I have become is the ultimate fulfillment of the sign on an ordinary license plate.

I love the symbolism of the "vehicle" related to the vehicle that is the body. When a 3 year lease period is up and I am due to return the car, it reminds me of the temporary state we are all in. You do not really own anything ever. We are in these bodies or forms of a vehicle that God has put us in, temporarily using them for our journey of life. When the time is up, we return this physical vehicle back to the rightful owner. After all, we are spiritual beings having a very temporary experience here on earth. Most people think the opposite is true. That is, physical beings having a spiritual experience. One of my favorite quotations of all time is by Meister Eckhart, "Time is what keeps the light from reaching us; there is no greater obstacle to God than time." My evolution to become a Now-ist is rooted solely in this truth. Time is what keeps the light from reaching us. We must disregard this illusion of time if we are going to find God. In my opinion, the only goal one should ever have is to seek the divine love of God, align one self with that focus, and live there always. This is the ultimate call of a Now-ist. All other "goals" will take care of themselves if you are primarily focused on the God that is closer than near and sooner than Now.

The ultimate modality of signs exists in the Holy Bible. Looking way beyond the life-changing parables of Jesus and the prophets, there is a holy gematria that can predict events from the past and the future. Gematria is a Kabbalistic method of interpreting the Hebrew scriptures by computing the numerical value of words, based on those of their constituent letters. You can enter words in the system and find related answers to all kinds of historic events. How can this just be a random coincidence? I maintain the "Bible Code," as it is called, is divine proof of signs that are always around us and with us. We just have to look with better eyes. The countless parables from the New Testament as well guide us to truth and a deeper understanding. If we can just pay attention and open our hearts and minds.

The miraculous arrangement of letters in the bible is a kind of "Holy Computer" if you will. This manual for life that God has created for his sons and daughters is a living and breathing book. It seems that most of us read and study the bible for divine guidance and inspiration for our life's situation. I find it even more incredible that this scripture has signs within the signs. The Bible Code, also known as the Torah Code, is a purported set of secret messages encoded within the Hebrew text of the Torah. This hidden code has been described as a method by which specific letters from the text can be selected to reveal an otherwise obscured message. The primary meaningful messages have been extracted using the Equidistant Letter Sequence (ELS) method. Many experts have tried to debunk this amazing discovery. I am reminded of a poignant quotation that addresses this very subject. "For those who believe, no proof is necessary. For those who don't believe, no proof is possible" (Stuart Chase, 1888-1985).

I am not one to go blindly following a whim or a quick-witted idea. I do believe in the feelings of our heart- that intuitive inspiration that takes us over when we really pay attention to the present moment event. If praying to God is our asking for guidance and assistance, then your intuition and inspiration about the subject is the answer. You must learn to pay attention to the signs. They are truly there just waiting for your discovery of them. It is almost like those times when a friend calls you up, late in the day after being out and about and asks, "Did you see me? I walked right past you in the store, and you didn't say hi or notice me."

Your reply, "Oh, I'm sorry. I was caught up in my head, thinking and consumed with thoughts about work, the kids, and my relationship." Life deals us this example routinely. You drift through the day not really paying attention to the greater play of life going on all around you. As I write these words, I am inspired to share with you, one of my favorite anecdotal examples from Dr. Wayne Dyer.

Thought is a kind of "currency" that we use throughout our day. Imagine you are using your thought or currency to purchase everything you want. You go to the store and see a huge, ugly rug that you would never want in your home. Never the less, you tell the sales person to send two of them to your house. You walk to the next store. There are lamps that match the hideous rugs you just purchased so you buy four of those. Finally, the last store reveals the worst set of table and chairs you have ever seen in your life. "Yes sir, please send that gross seating arrangement to my house." You get home and realize your house is full of everything you do not want.

The only conclusion you can come up with is "you are insane!" Why on earth would you spend your currency on everything you do not want? That is precisely what you are doing when you tell yourself that you are not good enough, you are not talented enough, you don't have enough money, or you are not beautiful enough. **Enough** already! You have to change the way you look at things for the things you look at to change (Dr. Wayne Dyer's philosophy).

I am encouraging you to pay very close attention to the signs that show up in your life. Adopt the inspired thoughts and consistently reinforce yourself:

"I am guided."

"The assistance or money I am seeking is on its way."

"This too shall pass."

"I am strong enough to get through this."

These kinds of thoughts and words will fill your house with the love and abundance you desire. "Home is where the heart is" you have heard. Make certain you are spending your heart's energy on what you want for your life. After all, the center of your universe is the heart. The feelings and emotions you experience charge your point of attraction. We only attract into our lives what we are, not what we want. Keep in mind this is not just positive thinking mumbo jumbo. You are not just saying words and expecting that to change your stars or point of attraction. Feeling it is the secret to charging your heart's magnetic attractor. When you say "I am strong!"- you feel it not only in your body, you feel it in the depth of your soul. Furthermore, in the book of Joel 3:10 it is said, "Let the weak say, I AM Strong." When you are proclaiming "I AM strong," you are stating the name of God. As it was revealed in Exodus 3:14, "And God said unto Moses, 'I AM that I AM' and He said, 'thus shalt thou say unto the children of Israel, I AM hath sent me unto you.'"

When you tell yourself "I AM strong," you are directly speaking from the God that you are. The name I AM is you. It is the name of God as well. One in being and One in word. John 1:1, "In the beginning was the Word, and the Word was with God, and the Word was God." This omnipotent, omnipresent, and omniscient truth should fill you with infinite love and the power of God almighty. When you fully embrace and realize this in being and in form, that you are GOD, nothing shall ever be impossible to you. Ever! You must re-read the last line of Exodus 3:14 just above, "*I AM* hath sent *ME* unto *YOU*." God tells Moses that he is sending Moses to the people. He says *I AM* the name of God and the name of Moses. For when you say *I AM* you are referring to yourself. In this story, Moses is given the task of leading his people to salvation. I believe that Moses is told to tell the "Children of Israel" that I AM has sent **me** unto **you**. When you deeply understand this sentence, you realize that I AM, the ME, and the YOU are all one in being. That realization is the salvation for all the children which means all of mankind. You will be lead out of any perceived evil or negativity in life. I AM is the ultimate self evident and self actualization of the Now-ist.

CHAPTER 7

CUT DOUBT WITH THE SHARPEST KNIFE

"Our doubts are traitors, and make us lose the
good we oft might win, by fearing to attempt."

— William Shakespeare

When I was twenty years old, a blessing came upon me. This gift,
if perceived by the thinking mind, might be construed as a curse.
I did attract it and that was what I thought I really wanted more than
anything else in the whole world at the time: a modeling contract in the
modeling capitol of the world. This was to be, in my narrowly-focused
mind, the one thing that would solve all the lacks in my life. The first seven
days in the "Big Apple" was a dream, living in a luxury hotel in downtown
Manhattan and feeling like a big shot. Once the honeymoon period was
over, I had my first taste of the biting "Sour Apple."

When I first arrived, my thoughts were positive and the beginning
looked promising. For an industry based on looks, I felt like I had this one
in the bag. Hard work was never a deterrent for me. I learned my work ethic
from my Pa and I was ready to dig in. However, the one reality that I did not
anticipate was the time it would take to "make it" there. My impression was
of quick success and flashy people. The day-in and day-out of the modeling
business was difficult work and not glamorous at all. As time eroded my
savings, the harsh actuality of life in Manhattan began to rear its ugly head.

My dear friend who lived there was kind enough to take me in. He rented a studio apartment right near Time Square. I slept on the floor and he did not charge me any rent. I was thankful for him; he barely had enough for himself, yet shared what he had with me. Work and money dwindled. After a few months, I was completely out of funds to sustain myself. This was the first time in my life I had ever gone hungry. I did not eat for five days straight. During this period, my doubt was the overwhelming ogre ruling my existence.

One day, I was soul-searching the streets of New York. I remembered the book I read by Norman Vincent Peale, *The Power of Positive Imaging.* This book was one of the reasons I was in the big city. The tools I learned reading it compelled me. He was a pastor there in the 50's and told many stories of powerful experiences he had in his church. My mission was to find that church. I was desperate and felt inspired to pray inside this historic building. After wandering and looking in phone books most of the day, I found it! There was a plaque with his name and dedication in the church. I was lost inside and could not even find the words to pray. As I knelt down in the pew, the Lord's Prayer came from my lips:

> Our Father, Who art in Heaven, hallowed be thy name. Thy kingdom come, thy will be done, on earth as it is in heaven. Give us this day, our daily bread and forgive us our trespasses as we forgive those who trespass against us. And lead us not into temptation, but deliver us from evil. For thine is the kingdom, the power and the glory, now and forever more, amen.

Precisely and desperately, I was praying for my "daily bread." The hunger I was experiencing was an overwhelming feeling of suffering and pain, both physically and emotionally. I asked for guidance and help. I truly did not know what to do. My mind kept repeating to me the last line of the Lord's Prayer, "For thine is the kingdom, the power and the glory, Now and forever more." This felt like the power that was going to take me out of this strife and suffering. God was going to help me, only I did not know how.

My magnanimous friend did not have enough money for food either. We both followed the routine of the day, only to meet each night and fall asleep in his tiny apartment hungry. The next day my fear, worry, and doubt was at an all-time high. "What am I doing here?" I questioned over and over again. I finally knew what true humility and meekness meant. The passage from the bible, "The meek shall inherit the earth" rang through my head. My imagination went to starving refugees and scenes of third-world children, naked and skeleton figured. I knew deep in my heart that all of this was happening for a reason. When I truly let go and let God in, the detachment from the ego occurred and everything changed. "On earth as it is in heaven" guided me. Also, "the meek shall inherit the earth" served me. I felt as meek as I possibly could, I thought. From that day on, I would trust and have faith in the power I was praying to.

My agent approached me the morning after my epiphany. He was extremely excited, handing me a scrap of paper with the address of the most powerful agent in the acting and modeling world at the time. "Mr. Schist" (we will call him) wanted to audition me for a soap opera. "The Lord has answered my prayers," I thought to myself. I instantly hit the pavement and started the long walk to the address in my hand. Once there, he greeted me with warm gestures and invited me inside. He wanted me to read with a female model that would be joining us momentarily. He offered me an alcoholic beverage while we awaited her arrival. An hour later, and no counter part to read the script with, "I don't know where she is," he states. Mr. Schist then tells me that he will read her part so the audition can take place. He asks me to take off my shirt because this character has to be fit and muscular. This was the first sign of trouble. We begin to read the scene and only a paragraph in, the air in the room went cold. I knew something was amiss. His face changed and I became the hunted. This was not an audition, but a set-up for this hairy, obese, balding pervert to take advantage of a struggling model. He knew that I was on to him and he started with offering me a part in his soap opera. When that did not work, money was his next attempt to acquire sex. As I grabbed my shirt, the first instinct I had was to punch him in the face. Something came over me and restrained me from that action. Not another look in his direction and I was out the front door.

"That was it!" and "I've had it!" I screamed. The Big Apple was the Big Asshole! I was gasping and crying as I walked down the street and at the end of my rope. Once I got back to the agency, my agent was laughing as I walked into his office. "This can be a tough business," he said. After a few harsh words, I was done. I recounted the story to my close friend and he equally laughed and thought it was a classic tale of trying to "Make It" in the Big Apple. Another confirmation of this foreign place's negativity and sleaze was the last straw.

A local comedian was a good friend of my room mate and he invited us to his stand-up show in Greenwich Village that night. After the drama and stress I had just endured, it appeared that God was balancing out my day. We had a good laugh at the show and the best surprise. A warm and hearty bowl of chili with a side of crackers was placed right in front of me! I can still see and taste that incredible gift from a stranger. After five days of no food this was the most amazing sign of hope. I ate it unhesitatingly like a ravaged beast in the jungle. The next day, I asked my brother Gib for the money to buy a plane ticket home. He generously wired the funds and to this day I have not been back to Manhattan.

The Signs will lead you out of doubt

The main reason I share this story is to illustrate the path out of doubt. This kind of event has occurred in everyone's life. We all have those moments when we feel lost and off our purpose. What we are attracting into our existence seems wrong and out of sorts. I point to the end of my New York modeling tale. There, I was lost and without hope, full of overwhelming doubt and no direction. Since then, my attention and intention focus on the power we all have within us- the I AM presence of all truth and direction. Once I had enough trial and tribulation, my instincts took me to the closest place and yet the furthest for most of us. Our very own power of intention, that is the I AM that I AM. Dr. Wayne Dyer, the great teacher of inspiration and motivation describes this power of intention best in his book by the same name:

> A sense of knowing, your infinite source of intention has no doubt. It knows and consequently it acts upon that knowing. This is what happens for you when you live on the active side of infinity. All doubt flies out of your heart forever. As an infinite being in a temporary human form, you'll identify yourself primarily on the

basis of your spiritual nature. This sense of knowing that comes from the active side of infinity means that you no longer think in terms of limits. You are the source. The source is unlimited, it knows no boundaries, it's endlessly expansive and endlessly abundant. This is what you are also, discarding doubt is a decision to reconnect to your original self. This is the mark of people who have lived self actualized lives. They think in no limit infinite ways. One of the no limit qualities is the ability to think and act as if what they'd like to have is already present. The power of intention is so doubt deficient, that when you're connected to it, your sense of knowing, sees what you'd like to have as already present. There are no contrary opinions what so ever.

My thinking mind was lost in material need and want in New York. The I Am presence was pushed down in me. My awareness was only resurrected once I became so despondent and distraught that I turned inward. We always have this power inside us. The key is to not wait until life has broken us and taken us to our knees. The active side of infinity that Dr. Wayne speaks of is that power we have to activate our knowing and powerful presence we truly are. Once you become aware of this infinite truth and experience it, doubt has no chance of controlling you. The awareness comes when you surrender to the moment of doubt. You come to the end and cease by resting in it.

The Sabbath- Resting in the End

In the Bible it is said that the Lord made the heavens, the earth, and all He created was good. He then rested on the Sabbath. The "Sabbath" means to cease or come to the end. When you come to the end of a long journey, you rest. You cease and refresh yourself from all the doing. In that end, you have let go of all that had transpired before you. Your doubts need time to survive. They live in the past and future. When you observe the Sabbath, you are at the end. You have ceased from doing and now become being. When you are thinking from the end, instead of about the end, you are resting in the Sabbath. Turn your back on the doubting five senses and overly thinking mind that create all negativity. Live in the assumption of your subjective hope. "The Sabbath was made for man, not man for the Sabbath" (Mark 2:27).

Let us say for example that you want to attract a desired outcome in your life. I had a person in my life that was doing wrong towards me. It was my intention to force this one to stop their behavior and succumb to my will and wishes. I acted in fearful ways and flooded our interactions with negativity and distain. Day-after-day, I wanted this person to change, finding myself constantly thinking and feeling the worst possible outcomes and scenarios. I would see what I did not want to happen daily. Thoughts and scenes of the very things I did not want to happen would overtake my feeling body. Even worse, I imagined it before I would drop off to sleep each night. You see, the subconscious mind only reacts to what you feel to be true. It is recorded as truth in your being. I was imagining the worst, feeling it in my body as real, and then resting in that feeling before I went to sleep. If there was ever the best way to stay stuck in what you do not want, this was it. They say addiction is never getting enough of what you do not want. Tragically, I was addicted to feeling wronged and hurt by this person. My lack of understanding how resting in the end with negative feelings was actually setting it in concrete. When I finally learned what the Sabbath was and acted on that end, that is when everything changed for me and this key person in my life. By imagining what I wanted it to look like at the end of all this suffering and strife, I would attract that outcome. Hence, each night before I fell asleep and first thing in the morning, I would use my imagination and observe the Sabbath. I would go to the end. I intentionally envisioned this beautiful person acting and being in perfect alignment with truth and honesty. I would feel it in my body and actually see details of the facial expressions while hearing kind words from a person set free from negative behaviors.

After a period of time, the most amazing change started to happen. The end that I was persistent in focussing on, actualized. I was stunned and over-joyed; I cried. Gradually this person, whom I have chosen to keep private, rose out of the ashes like a phoenix to the sun, when I rested in the end and truly observed the Sabbath. Using the feelings in a wonderful human imagination, my wish was fulfilled. To me, this poignant quotation from American poet and philosopher, Ralph Waldo Emerson (1803-1882) sums this up keenly, "To believe your own thoughts, to believe that what is true for you in your private heart is true for all man, that is genius."

In our traditional sense of the Sabbath, we are told to go to church. You observe the Sabbath by not working on Sunday. It is not holy to work on the day of rest. We are to feel guilty if we work or do not go to worship. Some can spend most of the day reading and taking in The Word and feel like they did their duty. They have observed the Sabbath. The most important part of the Sabbath is to rest in the Lord. The Lord is the I AM presence within you. You can spend all that Sunday listening and doing the things that people do on the "Sabbath" and never truly rest in the Lord. So many just sit there and allow the words from scripture to go right through them. They have not felt the message of the parables or stories revealed to them. The thinking mind wants things and events to keep it busy. When you honestly observe the Sabbath, you rest in the end. You do not need to feel like you did a duty out of obligation. The oneness that we are is God. When you can say I AM and know you are resting in the source that created you, you have cut your doubt with the sharpest of knives.

The Inner Body

Jesus of Nazareth stated, "I of my own self can do nothing. It is the father within me." Yet, we live our lives and feel like we are in control of the surroundings and our judgments. This is the sense of the outer body, taking in information and reacting to it with an instinctual reflex. This, however, is the key error in living with inertia and not awareness of being. The momentum of life easily takes our attention and tows us in and under the current on a river of living. How many times can you remember a moment when you started out with good intentions and before you knew it, you were lost in the physical world of human doings? You might have even told yourself, "Today I am going to stay positive and light in spirit." Then the phone rings. Bad news of one kind or another instantly transforms your good intentions into worry and stress. Your thinking mind leads you around like a wild horse fighting to be broken. You are caught between two states of being. You can choose to live in the outer world of form or the most powerful inner world of spirit.

You can connect to this inner world more rapidly than you might think. The inner body is always ready and willing to lead you out of struggle and strife. Much has been written and taught about meditation, breathing, prayer, and the like. In my experience of daily living, I find the connection to the inner body to be simple and quick. Contrarily, people think reading long prayers and remaining in deep meditation gains access to spirit. Life in this busy world appears to be speeding up, not slowing down. Instead of fighting this momentum, I have placed myself right in the middle of the action and take off in a flash of inner body awareness.

The Now-ist meditation feels and is experienced like this:

Close your eyes. Imagine yourself hovering above the planet. Once you are up there, feel what it is like to look down at your outer body and physical self on the earth. Then, take three deep breaths. Take the air in through your nose and slowly exhale out your mouth. For breath one, say this prayer line to your inner body, "I am altogether God and God is altogether me." Breath two states, "I AM that I AM the conquering presence in the Now." Breath three confirms, "I have nothing to do, only to be done." You want to speak the verse the entire duration of the breath. The meditation should only take less than one minute of physical time. I repeat this meditation regularly throughout the day when I find that my life's situation is attempting to pull me down and the outer body is becoming the primary focus. This simple prayer reconnects me to my inner body. Neville Goddard, the radical teacher of imagination and its true meaning, encourages us in his book *The Power of Unlimited Imagination* (1952):

> In the book of John, Jesus as a teacher makes this statement. 'Let not your heart be troubled, you believe in God, believe also in Me.' Then he adds this thought. 'It is expedient that I go, lest the comforter will not come.' Here we see a teaching that is seemingly taught from without, but is it necessary for your belief in any exterior teacher to disappear, for only then can the comforter within you, be found. There is only one cause, only one I AM. I the trinity, in unthinkable origin, am God the father, and in creative expression, am the son, for imagination is born of consciousness. I in universal interpretation, in infinite

immanency, in eternal procession, am God, the holy spirit. The real definition of immanence, is sooner than now and nearer than here. I am therefore the comforter. What could comfort you more than the knowledge that you don't have to wait for your dreams to come true. They are nearer than here and sooner than now. Let this knowledge be your comforter.

It is in this wisdom that I rest and realize the true power of the inner body's connection to divinity. You do not have to go through a process of mind body integration. This truth is in you, as you. As a Now-ist you connect using the inner body as the gateway to freedom from the outer world and its forces. You are more powerful than you know. All is as it should be when you detach from the worldly magnetism and seek the inner body's truth of oneness regularly.

Chapter 8

The Body of Oneness

---❦---

*"Take up one idea. Make that one idea your
life - think of it, dream of it, live on that idea.
Let the brain, muscles, nerves, every part of your
body, be full of that idea, and just leave every
other idea alone. This is the way to success."*

— Swami Vivekananda

Oneness... The thinking mind loves to take this concept and attempt to ruminate and cogitate on it. How can this simple word be the meaning to all that is and ever will be? In all religious and spiritual traditions, this one word circles back to the ultimate truth of singular focus and awareness of being. Yet, this word is only a beginning point of reference. Where it takes us is the journey back to our origin of being. It is said that the path to oneness is a journey without distance. Life will seemingly take you on a physical adventure, only to return to the place from which you began. The apparent circular logic in the concept of oneness is the perfect place to start this connection.

The first letter of the word is a clue. O is the never-ending shape that has no beginning or end. This letter appears in form and design in nature, time, and space. When we marry, the couple uses a ring to memorialize the union which is the symbol of infinite love and commitment to the partner's body and soul. Traditional belief, the *Vena amoris* vein runs directly from the fourth finger of the left hand to the heart. This theory has been cited in western cultures as one of the reasons the wedding ring is placed on the fourth finger. The heart is the center of the body's universe, the power station of connection to our love.

A binary code represents text, computer processor instructions, or other data using any two-symbol system, but often the binary number systems are 0 and 1. Here is our infinite symbol again in the computer world. These two existential symbols 0 and 1 are the impetus for creating this new plane of materiality. It literally takes 0 (representing infinity) and 1 (representing oneness) to manifest computer generated images, data and the like. It might be a stretch, however, when you combine these two symbols, you are in effect using *Oneness* to create this computer reality. I find this to be a clue in the thinking mind of creation. When you are *One*, you are connecting to the source power that created you. Oneness has no lack or scarcity. It is completely content and omnipotent. From this place of Oneness, you create the like conditions or circumstances of the energy that you are.

Human beings will also attract into their lives the like energy of the thoughts and feelings held consistently in that inner space of being. Case in point, a long held habitual pattern of thinking will mirror that pattern in materiality. For example, each time you consume your food of choice, do you take each bite of the meal in enjoyment? Or do you have feelings of guilt and regret? Do you think, "I should not be eating this- it will make me fat." The worry might continue with, "There are way too many carbs in this," looking at the container while chewing your food. The feelings and thoughts we harbor during a meal, shape the physical make-up of our bodies beginning at a cellular level.

In Dr. Bruce Lipton's book, *The Biology of Belief*, he reveals the astonishing truth that our thoughts and beliefs control the cellular health of our bodies. He has medically proven the impact fear and love have on our cells. "What quantum physics teaches us is that everything we thought was physical is not physical." He goes on to state, "If humans were to model the lifestyle displayed by healthy community of cells, our societies and our planet would be more peaceful and vital." In 2007, a Harvard study of hotel room attendants further confirmed this fact. The controlled study divided 84 room attendants working in seven different hotels into two groups. One group was told that the job they performed was considered a great work-out and burned lots of calories. Furthermore, this kind of exercise fulfilled the recommended daily activity levels required. The control group just went about their work as usual. Although neither group changed its behavior, the women who were conscious of their activity level experienced a significant drop in weight, blood pressure, body fat, waist-to-hip ratio and body-mass index in just four weeks. The control group experienced no improvements, despite engaging in the same physical activities. This study should serve as a wake-up call to the masses. Obesity in America has reached a staggering height. The World Health Organization estimates that 3/4 of the American population will likely be overweight or obese starting the year 2020. The latest figures from the CDC show that more than one-third (34.9% or 78.6 million) of U.S. adults are obese and 17% for children and adolescents aged 2–19 years.

Our thoughts and feelings about what we consume change the manner in which the food is converted in our bodies at a cellular level. If the vast population understood this fact, obesity rates would drop. Human beings want to feel good. Food can become a drug just like alcohol or smoking. The masses consume this drug in a desperate need for a quick fix seeking a respite once they eat the item of choice. Feelings of depression, loneliness, stress, anxiety, and worry all remain attached to the food being consumed. It appears to me that the rapid increase in obesity is directly related to mind-made negative states of being.

This fast-paced information age of instant gratification has created a society bent on rapid-doing, instead of being. I once heard a wonderful sermon by Father Charles at the Santa Barbara Mission. He coined a word that has stuck with me for years - "info-besity." Simply meaning, we are obese with information. Our minds do not have presence of being-ness. The information comes at us so rapidly that we consume it much like fast food, taking it in without awareness of how it is affecting our body and soul. Multi-tasking is a common way of life. It is almost as if society continually rewards us for the ability to do many things at once. The danger here is our lack of presence. A mind that cannot rest creates too much momentum. It is as if you park your car at the top of a hill and then walk to the bottom of the hill. You look back at your car, only to see that the brake has failed and down comes your car. The car crash is unavoidable due to the massive momentum built up. If we cannot learn to take a *break* from our thinking mind, this will be our fate as well. The "info-besity" will take us down the same road as the physically over-weight Americans.

Let's look at how this information age is affecting our bodies. Presence of being has very little to do with the fast-paced technological age we live in. When we focus our attention on our devices day-in and day-out, the thinking mind has little to no quality time with your inner being-ness. Our mind tends to chew on the problem or the tasks of the day. We might feel compelled to stop every once in a while to take a break. However, this rest usually means consuming some kind of temporary emotional state breaker, ironically more technology. I am convinced that if you can learn to enter the present moment consistently many times a day, you will attract into your life the like energy of peace and oneness that you are. The Now-ist state of being is the key to all abundance and true lasting wealth.

The Greek philosopher, Aristotle (384 BCE-322 BCE) proclaimed, "We are what we repeatedly do. Excellence, then, is not an act, but a habit." Once you understand what you are habitually doing during your daily routine, then you can engage in a more powerful choice of habit; thus, changing your point of attraction to peace and oneness. All energy is attracted to like energy. The vibration of peace and love is much greater than the vibration of fear and hate. Ask yourself the following questions in all honesty and heart-felt truth:

+ How many times a day do I feel stress and tension taking over my body?
+ What kind of habits do I have that attempt to break this stressful feeling?
+ Does worry and fear enter my mind consistently everyday?
+ Where is my stress and tension carried in my body?
+ Why have I continued this stress-filled habit?

According to the American Psychological Association,

Money, work and the economy continue to be the most frequently cited causes of stress for Americans, as they have every year for the past five years. In addition, a growing number of Americans are citing personal health and their family's health as a source of stress. Overall, people seem to recognize that stress can have an impact on health and well-being, but they do not necessarily take action to prevent stress or manage it well. Survey findings also suggest that time management may be a significant barrier preventing people from taking the necessary steps to improve their health.

As the APA stated, clearly the stress of Americans has dominated their existence. The lack of presence is the undoing of them. The world is not slowing down, it is indeed speeding up. If this dangerous trend is not interrupted, our society will continue to break down and dis-ease will proliferate.

Time is the culprit here. People look at time as a friend and as a foe. This split is part of the bigger problem. We have this crazy, bipolar relationship with time. The manic pace of life and need to get things done take us away from our authentic self. Usually the connection to time weighs heaviest on our sense of being. Depression can set in when time is not progressing in the manner we would like. Our focus is trapped in the world of doing and totally disregards the world of being. The habitual nature of human beings is rooted in progress and the need to be significant. Security and familiarity are also very important in one's life. The unknown is a threat to routine and the repetition that breeds comfort to the unaware. However, the unknown is precisely where you must go if you are to rid yourself of stress.

Your awareness of being is the best place to break the negative, habitual pattern. To pause and reset yourself many times a day is the key to ending your cycles of stress. The breath of life is the one thing that is always with you and ready to come to your rescue when you lose your way. One conscious breath taken many times a day is the new habit that will connect you to peace and well-being. When you make this practice a daily ritual, your life will change in ways you could only imagine. The following is another new ritual in body awareness and stress relief.

Ritual of Oneness

Make sure you are in a comfortable position. Sit in a chair with good posture. Your physiology is very important to start this ritual. A body with poor posture will not open the diaphragm enough to take in the necessary air for proper connection. Next, take three deep breaths at a very slow and deliberate pace. Each breath should relax you deeper. As you breathe, focus your imagination above the planet. See yourself hovering above the earth. Your arms are out to the side with the palms of your hands facing up. As you see yourself high above the planet, your body is in the shape of a cross. You are One with all that is. Your attention is not here on the earth. It is in the fathomless space of the universe. You cannot focus on your problems or stress. As you look around from that height, all you see is the gorgeous glow around your home planet and the deep black of space. The stars are the pin holes of light that shine through the black curtain of night. You are connected to the oneness that you are.

This ritual can also be done while in a standing position. Sometimes during my day, I will find my body and mind feeling tension and dis-ease. The attempts by the thinking mind can be very sneaky and underhanded. That is why your awareness of being is vital. You must check-in with your body and mind instinctually to know how you are feeling. When I feel tension and stress and I am in a place that is not ideal for sitting, I will simply find a quiet moment and stretch out my arms in a cross-like fashion. I am relaxed and my imagination places me miles above the earth. I am there with no attachment to time or worldly doing. My connection to oneness has become entirely natural; it feels like breathing. As I take in my breath, the stress and tension melt away and nothing can dissuade me from my being-ness. My life has become the central focus of my presence. The Now-ist sense of being is all that I AM. The connection to my body is more than just a physical connection to peace. It is a connection to the oneness of who I am and all that is.

Chapter 9

GOLF: Go On Life's Feeling

--- ✥ ---

"Ideas enveloped in feeling are creative
actions. Use your divine right wisely."

— Neville

I was taught the power of feeling as a creative action in the most surprising and unusual way. My journey has taken many turns that were not planned by my conscious mind. Most days, we think we are in control and have a plan or a schedule to guide us in a certain direction. I have always been that person who is well-organized and driven to accomplish what I have set out to do. I was taught at a young age that work ethic was paramount for success. I am humbly thankful my father taught me this tenet. However, it is in those moments when we are taken by a force that is closer than near and sooner than now that we expand in being-ness; I experienced what is called in the Zen tradition a satori, a flash of enlightenment. From that moment on, my life would never be the same.

Not that many years ago, I was a very frustrated person, completely caught up in doing and having more. I thought that accomplishing goal after goal was the key to happiness. This pursuit of "happiness" became my main focus in life. My central error was allowing my thinking to take over my being. I thought that if you work hard and practice the activities you love, you would "be" successful. Popular belief about the "10,000 Hour Rule" was not true for me. Pop-psych writer Malcolm Gladwell explains that it takes 10,000 hours of "deliberate practice" to be great in any field.

Ironically enough, it was around the time that I learned that connecting peacefully to the present moment would be more transforming than robotic practice hours.

I love golf. This challenging sport has become more than just a game to me. Never the one to take the road most traveled, I decided to go my own way. Typical golf enthusiasts work very hard, hitting range balls for hours and putting in time on the details. Putting, chipping, and other short game skills take years to perfect. To me, it just seemed arduous and time-consuming to spend all those hours practicing. What I really was enthused about was the adventure on the golf course. The unknown events just waiting to be experienced out there on the green ocean of possibility, drew me. My call to the game was the challenge. I have always been naturally athletic and relished sports. This game, however, seemed complex and difficult. I felt intrigued by first hitting a little white ball as hard as you could and then with more control and accuracy attempting to land it on a green. This game was wrought with unknowns. After you made the green, with careful finesse and focus, you putt it into a four-inch little hole.

I have always been fascinated by the unknowns of life. It just seems to be where the growth is. To not know what was going to happen each time I stepped up on that tee box was enticing to me. The real challenge appears when you have great expectations for the results and a thinking mind full of ideas about how to get there. Golf is a game of singular focus. When you first start to learn the game, the thrill of hitting a really good shot captivates your attention. The main problem is "How did I do that?" The game is counter intuitive in the beginning. You think by muscling that club with all of your might, you will produce the best result. However, the proper swing has a oneness about it that chooses you. Then from inspiration to deep frustration the unknown becomes known.

The Satori

I first picked up a golf club at the age of 21. After years of dabbling with the sport, it became more than just a game, once I moved to Santa Barbara. Being an autonomous person by nature, golf seemed to be the perfect blend of challenge, exercise, and oneness. Then, the most unusual thing starts to happen when you get better at the game. Your golf begins to mirror your attitude and energy of life. The quotation from Epictetus (AD 55-155), "Circumstances don't make the man, they only reveal him to himself" points squarely in the face of this game's truth. My challenges and demons were bubbling up and it was time to blow!

One day on a municipal golf course in sunny Santa Barbara, I was having an all-consuming, frustrating round. My life's situation was complicated. Fear and rancor had overcome me. It seemed like I had created a bad habit. I expected the game of golf to heal the wounds of life through some act of reductionism. However, on this day, all of that was about to change forever. Throwing my golf club after a terrible shot was a common outrage for me. I am not proud of these explosions of negativity that use to rule me on the course. There are fourteen clubs in the bag and it felt like I had thrown the lot. Then it happened. With only a hand-full of holes remaining in my round, my level of rage exploded. I threw down my entire bag after a poor shot, completely ready to walk off and give the game up forever. (These kinds of thoughts were whirling around my head the entire round.)

Then my consciousness shot me above the earth as if on a rocket ship. My thinking mind seemed to fry. Instantly, out of pure desperation, my awareness took me to a place of perfect peace. I was above the planet looking down on my "lower-self" standing in the fairway of the 15th hole of the golf course. I thought, "This is weird. How did I get up here?" I was floating high above and looking around at the gorgeous, blue line around the planet and taking in all the brilliant bright stars. I could even see satellites and the moon. Once I realized I could see myself on earth, the idea to witness the perfect golf shot came to me. I watched in amazement as I struck the golf ball from where I was in the fairway. As I made contact with the ball, I felt it in my body up there in space. It was the most pure and present feeling of contact I had ever felt hitting a shot. Then I watched in awe, as the ball traveled through the air and landed on the green about six feet short of the cup. With laser-like accuracy, the ball continued on and tracked right into the hole!

In utter shock and awe I thought, *I just saw and felt my "higher-self" hit the perfect golf shot.* Once my mind realized where I was and what had happened, I literally "peaced-out." My awareness came back to the solid ground of earth. With a smile and the spirit of adventure, I decided to take a deep breath and pick up my golf club. I was exactly 74 yards from the pin in the fairway standing over the ball with pure peace and confidence. I struck the ball with the same feeling of my higher-self. I watched the ball soar through the air tracking right at the pin. It then landed six feet short of the cup and went right into the hole! Ironically, I threw my club high in the air out of wondrous jubilation. The feeling of joy over-took my entire being and I was stunned and amazed.

What just happened? My mind was racing to try and make sense of this. With giddy-delight I walked to the green and plucked the ball out from the hole, holding it high into the air as if a crowd was watching and cheering me on. Looking at the ball and contemplating the force I just gained, it felt like I was a super hero that had acquired a new power. Laughing to myself I exclaimed, "I AM BLESSED MAN!" (My favorite super hero Batman was my template.) I do not remember another shot as I finished the remaining holes that day not caring what happened; I was in a place of pure joy. Walking on air was the closest feeling I could compare it to. When I returned to my car, I sat peacefully in the parking lot in contemplation and connection.

As I thought and replayed the shot in my head over and over again, it dawned on me. This is not just a golf experience. This is a life-changing process and practice. I became obsessed with reading higher consciousness books. I once read a quotation from Dr. Wayne Dyer that stated, "God will send you smarter people when you stop thinking in dumb ways." And so it was. Books and teaching that were in alignment with my higher awareness thoughts started to appear in my life. The most profound was the book by Eckhart Tolle titled *The Power of Now* (1999). It was revealed to me within its pages what had happened to me that day on the golf course. My higher-self was up above the planet looking down on my lower-self. The experience I had was called a satori in the Zen tradition. It was a flash of enlightenment, a sudden awakening to divinity, and an instant connection to oneness. As I learned more and studied liked a doctorate student in spirituality, this one satori became the impetus to changing my entire life.

The Power of Feeling it

The feeling supplies the fuel to the rocket ship that blasts you above the earth. In his book *Feeling is the Secret* (1951), Neville Goddard sums up the power and importance of feeling it in your body:

> The subconscious does not originate ideas but accepts as true those which the conscious mind feels to be true and in a way known only to itself objectifies the accepted ideas. Therefore, through his power to imagine and feel, and his freedom to choose the idea he will entertain, man has control over creation.

This is the power that will transform your life. Once you learn to use it, you will attract into your life what you are, instead of what you do not want. The key error most people make is getting caught up in the inertia and momentum of living. They are taken away by obsessive thinking and doing whatever is in front of them without awareness. When you consciously navigate your daily living, you gain a new habit of being that anchors you to the Now.

I began to use my "super power" to feel and imagine my new life. It even saved my daughter's life one fateful day on a cruise ship in the middle of the Pacific Ocean. Our family decided to take a cruise to Hawaii for the Christmas season. Fourteen days on a ship with our three and a half year old was an adventure. We were all very excited and had the best time. Playing the games and activities on the ship was a dream for us all, especially for our darling daughter. It was a wonderland at sea. My mother and father-in-law had a balcony cabin just across the hall from ours. Each night our little one would spend one night with us and one night with them. She is true fun and we wanted to share her joy. One day my mother-in-law got very sick. We all thought it was food poisoning. The next night our little girl stayed the night with them. She slept in bed with her grandmother and must have contracted germs. It turns out, the Norwalk virus was going around the ship and "Baba" as we called her, had it.

The next day our little one was ill, throwing up terribly. My wife and I spent all day in our cabin with Gianna trying to keep fluids in her and watch her temperature. As night fell, she was resting for a little while and then got sick again and again! We could not keep enough liquids in her. She would vomit them up. By morning, her fever was worse than ever. Surprisingly, this little trooper had such a great attitude. She would giggle and gush about Santa Claus landing his sleigh on the top deck of the ship. We called the emergency number for the hospital on the boat. They told us the doctors were not in until 8 a.m. With her fever spiking and no fluids for a couple hours, I scooped her up in my arms and started running down the hallways looking for the ship's hospital.

While I was racing around, the most terrifying thing happened. Our little angel went unconscious. She would not wake up. She was slipping away as I reached the door to the urgent care center on the ship. I banged on the door as hard as I could. A nurse met me and I instantly was guided to a hospital bed where I laid her down. She then started to shake and convulsed in seizure. My wife was crying and screaming at them. She was escorted out of the room and I was allowed to stay.

The calm that came over me the entire time in the hospital room was incredible. I only focused on what it felt like to see and feel our little girl, healthy and well again. I could see her playing on Christmas morning. I began to thank God for healing her in that moment while the doctors had a very concerned and worried look about them. Yet, I never lost my faith or hope. Minutes felt like hours and she laid unconscious and shaking. The ship was met by an ambulance at the dock as we ported in Kauai. I was even allowed to ride with her in the ambulance to the hospital. It was as if the calm serenity I was feeling had reached out to all around me. Once at the local hospital, a veteran pediatric doctor of forty years was taking care of our little sweet heart. He explained that she had a febrile seizure and would have to stay at the hospital for a couple of days. Just two hours into her stay at the hospital and the little champion seemed back to normal. She was laughing and being her usual light of the world, very tired, but alright.

The doctor wanted us to stay for two days in the hospital on Kauai and do a number of tests to check her brain. My wife and I were both concerned for her health, however she was energetic and back to normal within a few hours there. Our cruise would have been over if we stayed and we would have had to fly back to the main land. Against doctor's orders, we decided to get back on the ship. This however was not allowed as per ship procedure.

If a passenger was infected with Norwalk's virus, they did not want to infect more passengers by reentrance. As I rode in the taxi back to the ship, I imagined the chief officer in charge granting us back on the ship. I could feel the gratitude as we shook hands in thanksgiving. I felt the scene in my imagination as I hovered above the planet. Viewing the entire exchange, I saw us back on the ship in our cabin excited and relieved. When I sat down with the officer, his adamant recital of the rules of the ship seemed like law. Yet, I was never dissuaded from my end result. Later, my father-in-law said it was one of the most amazing reversals he had ever seen. My peace and patience with the repeated denials from the officer was the energy that transformed the meeting. Everyone was amazed by our reentrance to the ship and the fact that we were allowed to resume our Christmas vacation.

When you have an overwhelming desire and fuse it with the good of life, your feelings have the power to make your imagined scene a wish fulfilled. The great secret to manifestation is feeling. The scenes in your hopes have a power all their own. Yet, it is only when you charge that image with the rocket fuel of feeling that it has the power to materialize. Hope, as well, is very powerful in and of its self. It is a positive energy force for good. You take that hope and empower it with the feeling of the end. This is the super human power we all posses, yet few truly use. I am reminded of Dr. Wayne Dyer's sagacious question, "How could the God of one-ness ever recognize two-ness?" If I were going to the ship with only the hope that we would get back onboard, it would not have the power of the end and the power of the sabbath. When you go to the end in your imagination and **feel it**, you have created that reality in the world. It is only to the degree of your belief in that imaginal act, charged with feeling, that it materializes.

You must **Go On Life's Feelings** to create your dreams. I would like to create a planet of golfers. Yes, I love golf. Nevertheless, the "golfers" I am speaking of are these sentient beings that self direct the course of their lives with feeling in imaginal action. A life golfer would recognize a desire to change their point of attraction in life and know they have the power to do it. They could instinctively choose the end, wisely and consciously. Life gives you these opportunities daily. The choice is always there for you. Yet, does the momentum of the day control you? Be it good or bad? Most people do not have the awareness to correct the inertia of this habit. Remember, you have the ability right within you to manifest your wishes. Should you choose to focus your attention and feelings on the thing not working in your favor, there you go. You will rest in that feeling of negativity or just plain bad feelings to the conclusion of the event. It responds to you every time without fail.

When I need a reminder of what and who I AM, instantly, I remember the 46th Psalm, "Be still and know I AM God." This is the focus and energetic truth that brings me back home every time. As a GOLFER, I know there are 18 holes on the golf course. You have the number one and the number eight. "One" signifies the remembrance that we are all one. We come from oneness and we return to it. The anagram NOW-WON is the instant reconnecting word of the Now-ist. When you are in the Now, you have won. Next is the number eight. This is the symbol for infinity, no beginning and no end. It just keeps traveling as we do in a pattern or loop. Look at the number 18 and NOW see one infinite source!

Many holy books have this same symbolic number in them. The Hindu Bhagavad Gita has 18 chapters. The Tao Te Ching is made up of 81 verses. In Judaism, the word *chai* is numerically significant and the number *18* is universally synonymous with this word. Chai translated from Hebrew to English means life. Within the Jewish faith, chai possesses both numerical and symbolic meaning. It is meaningful to see that this is a very powerful number. When you become aware of the signs and symbols all around us, you begin to live life in child-like bewilderment, awe and wonder. If you suspend your disbelief and pay closer attention to what is present, you will reconnect with the infinite oneness that you are. I am inspired by the wise words of Ralph Waldo Emerson, "What lies behind us and what lies before us are tiny matters compared to what lies within us."

Another wink from the golf gods, I was playing at one of the most beautiful seaside courses in Mexico. I walked up to the eighth tee box and noticed a dove sitting peacefully on the grass. Instantly, I thought of the artist Prince and the song he wrote about doves. He had just passed away a few months earlier. I teed off and my drive ended up in a sand trap. Walking to the bunker, I had an idea that I wanted to write about. It was called the "active side of infinity." I realized this was not my idea, but Dr. Wayne Dyer's, which I had read about in one of his books. Immediately after this realization occurred, a Monarch butterfly flew by and brushed my face. I had not seen a Monarch butterfly the whole trip while in Cabo San Lucas.

The Monarch had been (and still is) showing up in my life at significant times ever since Dr. Wayne passed away. Then it hit me. All these were signs of synchronicity. These intensions were sent from heaven for my wisdom and connection to the divine souls that are my inspiration. Walking to the next hole, I was in such gratitude and awe, as I hovered above the eighth hole in reflection. It is from this vantage point that I have the most clarity and connection to the one infinite source that intended my here and now.

CHAPTER 10

BEWILDERMENT: CEREAL PARTIES AND WOLFIN'

"Sell your cleverness and purchase bewilderment."

— Rumi

I am a big kid. I realize when I announce that statement I am expressing God within me is a big kid. Fore the name of God is I AM that I AM. Just ask anyone that truly knows me. They would regale you with a great variety of examples and accounts of my child-like behavior. I have always been this way. When I was very young, my father would constantly have to stop my drumming at the dinner table. Spoons, knives, glasses, plates, or whatever was near me, that was my instrument. He would say over and over again, year after year, "Bill! Stop making that noise." It really did not matter which meal our big family was eating, the music in my heart and head never stopped. Now that I am older, the music in my "heart-head" just plays louder with a much better selection. My lovely wife knows. The good news is our daughter was born with the same wonderful gift. Our dinner table at home now features a duet.

Children are the masters of living in the moment. We are all born a Now-ist. Time finds a way to sink into you and trap us in this myriad of a time-bound self. After all, it is written in Matthew 18:3, "Truly I tell you, unless you change and become like little children, you will never enter the kingdom of heaven." The visionary Buckminster Fuller (1895-1983) stated this perfectly in his observation, "Everyone is born a genius, but the process of living de-geniuses them." I would like to take his word *de-geniuses* and further extrapolate with my child-like imagination. A little, three year old child is speaking this next sentence. "Da, Genie, Uses Us." I can hear a sweet voice pronouncing that word into a sentence.

The Genie Uses Us

We have all been used by the genie in the bottle. The genie is time and the bottle is our own human physical form. People are too focused on time and waiting for that beguiling temptress to grant our wishes. The hope that the genie will wait for us, or hurry up for us, is draining. Just ask yourself and consider these questions, declarations, and quotations:

"How much does time rule my thinking mind?"
"I don't have enough time to do that."
"How many times do I have to do that?"
"What if my time runs out?"
"I am sick of waiting all the time."
"Time is what we want most, but what we use worst."
—William Penn (1644-1718)

"Time and tide wait for no man."
—Geoffrey Chaucer (1343-1400)

Finally, this tyrant Time is going to kill us. Why is it that we all fight with time so blindly? Each one of us needs to look inside and see what this time-bound thinking has done to our society as a whole. Stress of course needs time to survive. It is catastrophic that millions have succumbed to the pressure of stress and worry. Keeping up with the Jones' is not getting any easier these days. The mantra of the ego is more. These are all the trappings of the genie:

"I have to compete with them!"
"I have to be better than them!"
"Being number one is what really matters."
"Working hard and making it, that is what will make me happy."

The truth is "time is an illusion," as Albert Einstein stated. The Now is the only place that this time clock will stop spinning. Children instinctively know this and play and live fully in their own present moment awareness. The next time that you see a bunch of children playing or laughing, notice how the past and future do not implicate the present moment gifts. Time does not exist. They only want to play and experience joy while in full-on-fun mode.

We can all learn from the simplest of things in life; truly these are the best. Nature of course is the easiest point of entrance to the Now. Luke 12:27, "Consider the lilies how they grow: they toil not, they spin not; and yet I say unto you, that Solomon in all his glory was not arrayed like one of these." The Now is eloquently displayed for us to imagine in this beautiful passage. No time here. Just peaceful acceptance of the universal abundance that is always here in the moment, if we will just focus on it.

During my busy work day, I may rush past a beautiful symbol in nature. Sometimes, I am stopped dead in my tracks by a flower. The closer I get to it and study the network of veins, layers, and vast colors, there it is, every time, the universe in its microcosmic representation. Heaven! Then, William Blake's (1757-1827) famous words will play in the background of my heart, "To see a world in a grain of sand and a heaven in a wild flower, hold infinity in the palm of your hand, and eternity in an hour." Blake was most definitely a Now-ist.

The Moment Man

Another wonderful way to enter the present moment consistently is by osmosis. That is by surrounding yourself with others that share your intention to consistently stay in the Now-ist state of being. The higher and faster vibration of the present moment energy wants to expand and grow. It does not want to be confined to tangent movements and peripheral activity which are lower energy sources. Its immensity, space, spreading out and reaching for the universe make all things possible. That is what I am illustrating here. I am blessed to have four beautiful sisters and the best brother in the world. God has further gifted me the "seventh sibling" as we all lovingly call him; he is my main man, Neal D. His actual name is Neal

Macomber. We have been best buddies for 35 years. I have fondly dubbed him: the "moment man."

Neal and I have endeavored to always be true to the moment. We attended Cheney High School in Washington state together. We were both athletes, "jocks" as the school's vernacular labeled us. I remember the first time we were confronted with peer pressure to drink at one of those "red cup" parties. We were at a friend's house with the parents out of town. The activities were centered around beer bongs, keg-stands, shotgunning beers, wine coolers, and the random pot smoking "stoners." Neal D and I were not these kinds of teenagers. We had an original idea when confronted with this lower energy activity.

The Cereal Party

Neal and I were riffing… *what if, we invited a bunch of friends over to your parent's house and served Lucky Charms, Captain Crunch, Frosted Flakes, Honey Nut Cherrios, and Life (my personal favorite) with chocolate milk, played loud music, and rocked a "Cereal Party?"* We instantly came up with the code name for the party: CP! High school students desperately want to be cool and blend in with friends and peers. Following the masses is quite common when the need to fit in is paramount. Our idea came from the place of not needing to fit in with "cool kids." We loved the state of mind we lived in every moment. Why in God's name, literally, would we want to get drunk and leave this perfect state of bliss! Yet, I did understand why students want to drink and hook up with each other. "Liquid courage" was the main driver at these parties. Everyone just wanted to escape and not be in their usual state of mind. The moment man and I completely recognized this and felt called to offer up a healthier and safer alternative, and thus, the CP was born!

This became a sort of viral adventure at school. Our classmates would talk it up at school and even created a hand signal like a secret society. To make the sign, you take your left hand and make a C shape. Then you hold your right hand flat with the palm facing left and bring the two together with the C shape at the top of your right hand. This is the secret CP hand signal. Kids would be in class during a lecture or a test and shoot the hand signal over to a friend, confirming it was on for Friday night. The idea became a novelty and safe place and continues to grow. My wife, a high school teacher, is dedicated to her "scholars" as she calls them. (Her passion was recognized with the prestigious County Teacher of the Year award). When she took our idea and introduced the CP to her English class, they loved it! The moment man and I are inspired that this wonderful tradition still lives on in high schools today.

Wolfin'

One Halloween season during my sophomore year in high school, Neal invited me to work in the very scary Hagle's House of Horrors haunted house. His sister Sherry was a talented seamstress and created our frightful Timberwolf costumes out of gray fur-like material. Inspired by her design, we then found the scariest wolf masks and claws imaginable. We designed tennis shoe wolf feet to round out the realistic look. We were stationed in the Timberwolf forrest part of the haunted house and would jump out just when the patrons would least expect it. Night after night for the weeks leading up to Halloween, we loved it. Giving people a scare was a thrilling and alive way to help them enter the present moment. When you stop and think about it, being scared or shocked in a moment like that, truly forces all of your attention and focus to exist only in the present moment. Perhaps that was the red herring to my ultimate calling as a Now-ist.

William Blake's observation speaks true, "Death is the best thing in life. There is nothing in life like death, but people take such a long time in dying. At least, their neighbors never see them rise from the grave." One has to die to the past or future every single moment to live Now. It reminds me of Halloween and the one night a year that people all over the world attempt to live in the present moment. People escape the worldly roles they all play. Just for one day, the inner child gets to run free and imagination rules the night. Children do this more passionately than the vast majority of adults. Fore if you do so, the best thing in life is death. Imagine if you lived your life this way. What could you be, do, have, become, and attract into your life? This is the central message of a Now-ist. Death! I know it sounds morbid or perhaps misunderstood my billions of human beings, but there it is. You must die, metaphorically, to the past and future every moment in life if you are going to live life to its fullest. You must embrace the death as the catalyst for that awareness. The last line of Blake's quotation takes my imagination to Michael Jackson's iconic "Thriller" video, the best Halloween music video ever made! The zombies come out of the graveyard and start to roam the streets. They all surround the pop-star and his back is facing the scene. When he reappears he is then one of them and they all break out in one of the most famous dance numbers of all time, (osmosis in the Now) joining the collective present moment awareness of the same kind and becoming One. Won! Now! Blake's, "...at least their neighbors never see them rise from the grave" comes true to show the eternal Now. I am optimistic that more and more neighbors will rise from their tombs of the scull and of the mind, so that all can see them free of the past and future graveyards.

Channel the Wolf

Neal D and I also share an incredibly deep love of music. This passion increases as the years go by. My inspiration to perform and write music started at an early age. I have pursued music as a career many, many times in my life. One stretch of about three years was particularly exciting. My other musical buddy DG and I were over-joyed to hear about a new television singing competition about to open for auditions. He and I had hoped that one day a competition would offer aspiring singers over 29 years old a shot at the "big time." Audition day had come and we were ready to take it to them. DG and I had auditioned multiple times in many different cities with varying levels of success. The first year was the best. Out of 16,000 contestants, we made it to the top 300 to 400. I remember all the auditions vividly. However, the most exciting part for me was the connections with all the other hopefuls. It was truly meaningful and magical to wait for hours time after time with the powerful collective energy that many people could generate through hope. I feel like my interacting and talking with nervous and even crying contestants to give them peace and confidence was the ultimate calling for my inspiration to keep trying to "make it." I was able to help countless people crush their fears and believe in themselves, revealing to them inspirational signs and synchronicity all around them if they would just open their hearts and pay attention.

On the last year of the show, Neal was inspired to travel to auditions with DG and me. He was excited to be part of the powerful energy we described. His main focus was to support us and cheer us on. He would audition as well, but his heart's intention was to help others and entertain. Throughout the multiple auditions and two different cities, Neal was there to support the other aspiring singers with dissipating their fears and nerves, even smile and enjoy the process. He always came from the place of, *how can I serve these people in this adventure?*

Months prior, I was sharing with him the wisdom I had gleaned from years of studying and feeding this spiritual hunger of mine.

"Thoughts are things."

"Energy flows where focus goes."

"Now is the only moment and power you have to change your life."

"Imagination is the greatest gift God has given you."

Neal was experiencing challenges in many areas of his life and we had frequent deep conversations about how to change it all, by thinking from the end, instead of about the end.

Fast forward to the moment man's big time debut to the world. Neal had one of the most memorable auditions of the show's season that year. DG, my daughter, and many friends were there in the auditorium for the national television taping of Neal's all-out, powerhouse performance. When he finished, over 4,000 people were on their feet cheering and screaming from the excitement he generated while singing, dancing, smiling, and entertaining on and off that stage. Later, he would sign autographs and eventually the show would air for 20 million viewers. His audition was viewed on the internet by 750,000 people and counting! When I asked him later how he did it, he said, "I just channeled the Wolf." He further expanded by sharing with me the spiritual charge he got right before he went on stage. He entered the present moment unlike any time in his life. He displayed his most authentic self in the moment. He had such organic fun that he did not focus on the outcome. His energy was omnipresent awareness. He truly was the "moment man." The "wolf" was his pure self and nothing else could even enter his being; thus, all positivity was attracted to him.

PIF Packs: Pay-It-Forward

Compassion is fire in my heart. I am made up of the deepest feelings of compassion for all of my fellow souls on planet earth. It rules my being and fills me with such contentment when I can be of service to another. Living in truth is the most connected you can be with another person. Like the book of Matthew teaches, "out of the mouth of babes." Little children instinctively know when you connect with them. They speak freely without any barriers. I have always loved children. It is purely who I Am. I get them and they get me. Communication is effortless and they instantly bring me fully into the present moment. When our little daughter was about three years old, I had the best idea. It was imperative that I teach our sweet child the necessity of giving and being of service to others. My inspiration gave way to a catalytic practice that has shaped our daughter's heart, soul, and spirit.

One day after picking up our little one from pre-school, I noticed a man on the street corner at a stop sign. I had played golf earlier that day and had a drink and few snacks left over. They were still on the passenger seat in a small bag from the store. I rolled the window down and handed it to the very dirty and bearded man. He greeted me with excitement and blurted out, "You just saved my life!" I wished him all the best and replied, "God bless you man." While driving away I was filled with joy and soulful abundance. Miles down the road with a contemplative voice our little angel said, "Good Dadda." I responded, "Yes, thank you sweetheart." Then, it hit me and I recalled the Harvard study that I read months before.

Professors at Harvard conducted a study (2010) to measure the serotonin levels in individuals that offered a stranger an act of kindness. They then measured the levels of the recipient of the generosity. The study concluded that the serotonin levels raised significantly in each the giver and the receiver. However, the best part of this scientific study was revealed when they also measured the serotonin of a witness to the act of kindness. Incredibly, the bystanders' serotonin increased the same amount as the giver and the recipient! This is how you change the world. Serotonin makes you feel good. A spiritual truth, "Feeling good and feeling God are the same." If we can all be focused on being in kind service to one another, exponential growth will occur and it will all happen by example, with no ego-ic credit.

When I entered back into the present moment with my daughter in the car, I realized what I could do to teach my daughter this lesson regularly. I loved the movie *Pay it Forward*. I instantly had the idea for "Pay it Forward Packs" and imagined how my daughter and I could make and give them. This all happened before we arrived home from pre-school that day. Parking my car it was all so clear and already created in my imagination. We would call them PIF Packs. This was my daughter's first introduction to an acronym.

The next day we went to the store and purchased drinks, socks, protein bars, candy, crackers, beef jerky, and gum. Our sweet daughter was excited to shop for these items and filled the store with her joy. I let her pick them out and feel the wonderful feelings of preparing to give perfect strangers these gifts. The attendant at the check-out counter commented on all the goodies and my little one replied, "We're gonna do good!" When we arrived home, the ping-pong table was instantly converted into a make-shift assembly line. "Just like Santa's workshop," my little pumpkin proclaimed. *Now for the bags to put these treasures in*, I thought to myself. Years of playing in charity golf events filled my garage with a great number of empty gift bags. This was the perfect container for the PIF Packs!

My little elf and I made about thirty PIF Packs. We vowed to always have one in the car so when we saw a person in need we could be of service. A little voice then chimed in, "Can I put somefin' in the PIF Pack?"

"What do you have in mind?" I asked.

"I can draw a picture," Pumpkin replied.

"Of course, whatever makes you feel good sweetie. What if we put some nice words in there- like a little note?"

She excitedly said, "Yes, Yes!"

"What would you want to say to help people?"

"Um, aaa, oh… I hope this brings you Hope!"

I swooped her up in my arms and gave her the biggest hug. "You are so wonderful, Sunshine," I whispered in her ear. Naturally, we printed up little strips of paper with that phrase and placed one in every bag. "Out of the mouth of babes" indeed!

Years later, my wife and I were in a parent teacher conference with our daughter's third grade teacher. After the review, she asked me what we did to raise such a compassionate and caring child. She said that in all her years of teaching she had never taught a student with more genuine enthusiasm and joy for others. "Another student will be having a tough day and Gianna is the first to come to their aid," she said. "Additionally, a classmate will achieve an award and GiGi will be the loudest one cheering their accomplishment. If something is out of place or the classroom is in need of a cleaning up, she is the very first one to chip in. What on earth did you do?" she asked again. I started my explanation with the Harvard study on serotonin. She was deeply fascinated by such a concept; it had never occurred to her in her many years of teaching Catholic school. Once I shared the PIF Pack's genesis, I could see the light bulb blink in her imagination. "We should do that here at our school," she gleefully announced. We then spent the next thirty minutes on what that would look like at a school level and the spark of compassion was growing to inflame an entire school. Needless to say, Catholic schools week had its first school-family-neighborhood-city, PIF Pack experience.

Our beloved Dr. Wayne Dyer spoke of a spark of God living in each of us that starts small and can grow. If we fan that flame, it will grow from a flicker to a flame to a fire! Dr. Wayne connected and quoted Elizabeth Barrett Browning (1806-1861), "Earth's crammed with heaven, and every common bush afire with God; but only he who sees, takes off his shoes - The rest sit round it and pluck blackberries." Either you can see just a bush or you can know and act in alignment to the presence of divinity.

Stuff Sick

The complete divine connection of children is the main reason I feel called to their wisdom. Many a sage, speak of life being asleep as we grow older and older. We are all born fully awake and each passing day we sleep deeper and deeper in the not so comfortable bed that is the world. Jesus said, "I am in the world but not of the world." I find it crazy that more and more fellow human beings get lost in the raging river of life. One of my favorite songs of all time is "Crazy" by the artist Seal. The most powerful lyric he sings is, "In a sky full of people only some want to fly, isn't that Crazy?" We all have this child inside us. Crazy behavior is displayed in life when we forget to dream in that child-like imagination that is our birthright. The insanity of growing older is the focus on doing to gain more recognition, separation, and the so-called all important "stuff."

This pursuit of things has driven the world crazy. Lao Tzu describes the world of the 10,000 things. This world has nothing to do with truth of your being. Your true authentic self lives, breathes, and has its being in the connection to the divine. The I AM presence is the boat that buoys us to safety, allowing us to navigate the rapids of this roaring river and through the world of the 10,000 things.

Our incredible daughter has the best imagination. One day she and I were cleaning out her room. She stopped for a second and looked right at me and said, "Daddy, I have so much stuff. I think I am "stuff sick." I then thought to myself, *What a fitting term to describe the epidemic that has overcome the world!* We sat on her bed and I knew this was an opportune and ripe time to elaborate on her brilliant idea, taking this precious time to explain to her the profundity of her thought. I allowed her to feel what it felt like to be surrounded by all the "stuff" filling her room and having no attachment to it. Furthermore, I reminded her of a bedtime story that I imagined for her some time earlier in the year.

Most nights before our sweet little girl is asleep, I sing her a song I wrote or create an extemporaneous story for her from my imagination. One night, I had the inspiration for a story and created an entire parable in the moment. It was called "The Land of Experia!" In the story, a little girl who lives in the mountains of Italy, named Sally Simpsioni, was cleaning out her room. She was inspired to give away half of the toys from her large toy chest and bring them down to the village for the less fortunate children. After clearing the chest of half the toys, she was rather tired and sat down to take a rest. She leaned against the toy chest, now half empty, and it slid out from under her further down the wall. When she picked herself up off the floor, she noticed a bright little light. It almost looked like a tiny bulb from a Christmas tree. Sally got down on her hands and knees to investigate this strange light. She got her face so close to the light that something shot out from it and hit her right on the nose. She shook her head and crossed her eyes to see what was on her face. A voice cried out, "Are you Sally Simpsioni!?"

"Why yes, who are you?"

"You can call me Lady Bug," the insect replied. "I have been ordered by the king of Experia to bring you with me right away."

"I can't fit through that tiny hole with you," Sally said.

"Well, of course not. You have to come with me to see the Blue Fairy in the forest first. She will shrink you down to size."

So Sally followed Lady Bug down the hill through the woods to find the fairy. She then tapped her wand on Sally's head and reduced her size to smaller than Lady Bug.

The story then takes Sally and Lady Bug through the hole in the wall to the Land of Experia. In this incredibly magical place, a legend was told of a very special, little girl that could save the land from an evil witch, who locked the king's daughter in a tower with no way out. This pure-hearted child was the only one who could pass through a tiny crack in the tower wall to save the princess. Once another human entered the room in the tower a door would open and the Princess would be free.

Sally does as the king requests and frees the Princess from the tower. The evil witch is banished from the land, forever. Sally is the heroin and returns home back through the tiny hole in the wall and retains her power to shrink down to smaller than Lady Bug. When she is back in her room, the realization of the fantastic experience is only due to the inspiration of giving and heart-felt love for others.

When I concluded this story for the first time, my daughter was too enthralled to fall asleep. Staying awake in our daily comings and goings is the simplest yet most difficult task. If all of us could just follow the signs of our lives. Pay attention, be astonished, and tell other people about the inspiration that is always there throughout our common hours each and every day. Synchronistic events occur in our present moments that can change our very existence! Do not miss the connection to that homeless, elderly, or lonely person in need on the street. Do not let the daily inertia that hypnotizes us into sleep and right past the opportune spark that could light the fire of change for each one of us. Jesus said it best in Luke 6:38, "Give, and it will be given to you. A good measure, pressed down, shaken together and running over, will be poured into your lap. For with the measure you use, it will be measured to you." Thankfully, our daughter learned this life lesson sooner than most.

CHAPTER 11

B.T. THE BI-TERRESTRIAL

---❦---

"My kingdom is not of this world. If it were, my
servants would fight to prevent my arrest by the Jewish
leaders. But now my kingdom is from another place."

— John 18:36

The year was 1982. The world was mesmerized by a little three-foot tall creature from another planet named E.T. The movie, *E.T. the Extra-Terrestrial* was the summer's block buster. I remember that time and the impact the movie had on people. The story was compelling and imaginative. Movie-goers could not help but feel compassion and empathy for the little alien who got lost and was trying to get back home. He had help, however. His new buddy Elliot who discovered him was doing his best to assist the foreigner. E.T. could not live in our world. His biology was not made to stay on earth very long. He started to die and the adults were trying to help E.T. However, the one that saved his life was young Elliot. He smuggled him out of the medical tent and into the basket on the front of his bike. The now iconic image of E.T. and Elliot flying past the moon thrills the heart. E.T. elevated them so that they could fly to the waiting spaceship of his family. The tear-filled goodbye sends E.T. back home with a lasting hug from Elliot.

We are that boy and we are that alien trying to get back home to a place of peace and serenity. American poet E.E. Cummings (1894-1962) wrote about our struggle to be an individual in a society that perpetuates mainstream living. "To be nobody but yourself in a world that is doing its best day and night to make you like everybody else means to fight the hardest battle which any human being can fight and never stop fighting." It is as if we are in this never-ending battle with the world and our authentic self. We are held to the fight by a symbolic type of gravity. The gravity of the planet is both a blessing and a curse. In the practical sense, it holds us and all things to the earth. However, the magnetic pull of the ego is usually the more powerful force here. The ego's magnetic mantra is, "I am what I have. I am what I do. I have to compete. I am separate from what's missing in my life." Most erroneously, "I am separate from God." The world constantly tells you that you are not enough. The advertisements and media are endlessly pitching to you, always preying on your sense of having to measure up and compete with the "Jones." We are told, "You have to go to this school to get the best education." Brain-washing ideas about college, career path, clothing, perfume, jewelry, shoes, and the list continues.

"I am this, I am that," the ego tells you. The biggest disconnection is the irony of the ego's "I am" statements, "I am what I have. I am what I do. I am what people think of me. I am separate from God." We know that Moses was told the name of God in just one place in the bible- at the burning bush on Mount Sinai. God told Moses that his name was "I Am that I Am," and that is the name of God for all generations. The EGO attempts to "Edge God Out" as Dr. Wayne Dyer cleverly labeled this acronym. To state "I am" a material thing such as a reputation or a physical item is the greatest error. Jesus tells us in John 8:23, "You are from below; I am from above. You are of this world; I am not of this world." To be a "Bi-Terrestrial" is the existential key that Jesus is sharing with us here. You must exist in the world of divine spiritual imagination and the world of physical form. To live on this earth you move and breathe and have your being. There needs to be a separation and a union simultaneously. I love this quotation from Rumi that points to the duality of living:

> Being desirable means being comfortable with your own ambiguity. The most ambiguous reality is that we are flesh and spirit at the same time. Within everyone there is light and shadow, good and evil, love and hate. In order to be truthful, you must embrace your total being. A person who exhibits both positive and negative qualities, strengths and weaknesses is not flawed, but complete.

If human beings can reconcile this mystery within themselves, life will become a balanced abundant existence. The counter intuitiveness of life can seem confusing and disjointed. This is why being a Now-ist is essential to living. One must learn to live in the physical restraints of time and the infinite oneness of the spirit. When you can be in the present moment with all of its variety and challenge, knowing that you are ONE, you have just mastered your life. Time, space, and circumstance will not hold sway over you. You will meet each day with the same content feeling of knowing your truth. When a challenge presents itself, the "Bi-Terrestrial" that is you, will respond with the awareness of the earth and the stars. With the divine guidance that is your origin and never-ending resting place, your life will be what it is, with no resistance from the ego and its false sense of self.

When I was a teenager, the world had its claws firmly around my neck. It constantly choked out the spirit world within me. My divine focus was at war with wanting desperately to fit in and stand out. My father did his very best to provide for six children in the midst of divorce. When I wanted more expensive items, my meager bus boy or sales clerk salary was not sufficient. Hence, while in the wretched worldly grip, my ego stole whatever it wanted. One day while working as a sales person at a men's clothing store, I decided to go on a shopping spree after the store closed for the day. It was about nine o'clock and I was the only closer that night. Once the front gate was locked and the lights went out, I proceeded to fill two large, black trash bags with all kinds of merchandise. I must have stolen two thousand dollars worth of the store's goods. After my looting was complete, I snuck the two bags out the service door to the mall and off I went.

The following day, I had the morning shift. Around noon, I was feeling like a cat that ate the canary. Then the guilt set in. My heart was rock heavy and I was ashamed of my overwhelming need to fit in. *What is wrong with me? I am so much better than this kind of criminal behavior,* I thought to myself. Then the most amazing thing happened to me. I will never forget the feeling of what occurred next. Around one o'clock, two young men about my age walked into the store. They had only come in a couple of steps when I noticed their perfectly-pressed, white short-sleeved dress shirts with black name plates. You see, I was raised Mormon and I instantly knew that these were two missionaries out "tracting." (This was a term used by The Church of Jesus Christ of Latter-day Saints for missionaries spreading the church's message out into the world.) My dear friend Curtis was Mormon and he told me all about his mission in Lima Peru.

The two missionaries seemed to walk in slow motion towards me. Once they were about twenty feet away from me, my heart filled with the most amazing warmth and magical feeling. It was as if a warm shower was turned on inside my entire body. I had only felt this feeling once before in my lifetime. At thirteen years old, I was baptized in the Mormon Church. After the full body immersion in the font, I dried off and was sitting in a room alone before rejoining my family. The same incredible connection to the spirit filled my entire being with love and the fire from heaven. My heart immediately knew what this experience was. The Holy Spirit was feeling and recognizing the Holy Spirit in the missionaries. They did not utter a word until they were standing directly in front of me at the sales counter. To this day, I do not even remember what words we exchanged. This was one of the most powerful spiritual experiences of my entire life, the impetus to my mission on earth! My unquenchable spiritual hunger would begin on this day.

About a week later, a beautiful older woman approached me at the same counter as the missionaries. She asked me if I had ever modeled before, introducing herself as the owner of a prominent modeling agency in town. I proceeded to make small talk with her. A few days later, I was shooting with a professional photographer in her studio downtown. My career as a professional model was off and running. The world of fashion and aesthetic focus became the main crux of my existence. After becoming a big fish in the little pond of Spokane, Washington's modeling world, my wonderful modeling agent/owner encouraged me to fly to New York City and enter the world's largest modeling and talent contest. While in the "Big Apple," I was given the experience of what it is like to really be "in the world." The high pace of bold-faced, worldly living was more than my soul could bare. In a span of months, I was given the highest high and lowest low. By the end of my journey, I was hungry, broken, and penniless.

In hindsight, I am thankful for these experiences. I was blessed with first-hand "real-life" worldly living. My awareness of living in the world and not of the world was completely shaped while in Manhattan. It felt like I went through a time machine. God gave me a glimpse into the truth of who I really am. I feel fortunate to have gone through it so quickly. Never could

I have imagined learning these universal lessons in the manner delivered. Once my life's situation was through with me, it let go. At this point, I feel that most people have two choices: "you can't beat 'em, so let's join 'em" or "become One with God."

When the masses follow the way of the world, it is like a train on a track. We are all riding along, not aware of the choice we have to flip the switch and choose a different direction of travel. The certainty and strange comfort the train provides is magnetic and unconscious. It seems like human nature to want to fit in and be just like everybody else. I did ride the subway while I was modeling in New York. The faces I looked into while on the train were drawn and seemed beaten by the world. This lasting image reminds me of a clever comparison Tony Robbins made to boxes and human beings. "We sleep in our box-shaped beds. We go to work in our boxcars. We work in our box work space while looking at a box computer. We go home and look at a box television and then go to the refrigerator for a cylinder to create some variety." When I remember those faces on the subway train, this was the collective feeling. It might sound cliche, but thinking "outside of the box" is the only way to freedom from group think. You are now left with your other choice. "Become One with God."

When the world is done with you, it does not look back and wait for an answer. We all have these moments in our lives that shape our destiny. This choice is usually much more difficult to make. It means bucking the world and going it alone, so to speak. You might even be so conditioned that it feels counterintuitive to leave the world of "10,000 things," as Lao Tzu calls it. The familiarity the world provides is speciously attractive. Do not get sucked into the trap. Remember this philosophy by Thich Nhat Hanh, "There is no way to happiness, happiness is the way." To feel good, is to feel God. We are feeling beings. When you get to that moment in your life when you are ready to make that choice, always remember, the thought will be the lie and the feeling will be the truth. Arguably the most brilliant thinker of the 20th century was Albert Einstein. He poignantly encourages us to deal with this choice in his quotation, "There are only two ways to live your life. One is as though nothing is a miracle. The other is as though everything is a miracle."

Life will give you whatever you focus on. The saying, "energy flows where your focus goes," is pointing you in the direction of your life. Via the

Law of Attraction, this is an eminent fact. Should you choose to focus your attention on the things of the world, you will gain the worldly possessions you desire. You will identify with them and build yourself an ego-based existence. After all, the mantra of the ego is, "I am what I have, I am what I do, and I am what people think of me." You will also be dominated by having to ensure them and worry about them being stolen, lost, or destroyed. Yes, if you choose to completely identify with the world of the 10,000 things, you will be held to the restraints of that choice.

The animated movie *Aladdin* illustrates this point perfectly. In one of the final scenes of the movie, the villain steals Aladdin's lamp. After some coaxing from Aladdin, he realizes that if he wants to make the most out of his final wish, he should ask to be the most powerful genie in the universe. The genie grants the antagonist his wish and he becomes this enormous powerful genie. There is only one problem. He is bound by the curse of the lamp. All of his massive power is confined to an itty-bitty lamp. He is restrained by the very thing he obsessed over, to be in the world and not of the world. This is the challenge we all face daily. To be a Bi-Terrestrial is to live in oneness with that duality, to fuse the higher-self and lower-self in one being and to have your imagination firmly in your heart. You hover above planet earth seeing your lower-self with all of its doing. The higher-self is guiding you all along the way of your desire, tempering you with the truth about materialism, never allowing to be overtaken by the world and its allure. You make decisions and those choices shape your life. Always focus on the higher good and therefore God.

CHAPTER 12

THE REAL-ATION-SHIP: SINK OR SAIL

---◆---

"The law of floatation was not discovered by the
contemplation of the sinking of things... but by
contemplating the floating of things which floated
naturally, and then intelligently asking why they did so."

— Thomas Troward

Success leaves clues. It makes perfect sense to not reinvent the wheel. When one person has a loving connection or union with another, it is logical to repeat the steps to that outcome. Thomas Troward (1847-1916), an English author, observes the mind-set that an optimistic person would endeavor to take when charged with inspiration. I imagine that the team at NASA never thought, *We cannot go to the moon, it is just too far away.* Likewise, Christopher Columbus' focus was not on an unknown adventure that just might yield the discovery of the new world. Energy flows where your focus goes. We get what we think about all day and all night long. Yet, in a relationship, this energy more often than not, seems to get misguided and focused on what we do not want. Common pronouncements sound like this:

"I am the victim here."
"You never think about me!"
"How could you do this to me?"
"You are so selfish and obviously do not care about my feelings."

The one-sided energy of these kinds of internal or external statements ring true for human beings. There is a needy me that is wronged or mistreated. I must defend myself and stand up to this kind of abuse. This is a "normal" response to protect ourselves. We want pleasure and do not want pain. We instinctively respond to confrontation, be it emotional, social, spiritual, and especially individual. One takes up a position instantly out of justification or renunciation in a relationship. The force or counterforce is the common seesaw effect of our human drive to connect with another. Now ask yourself: how has this "normal" mind-set helped you through the challenges in your relationships? Did this position you took out of resistance and reflex help you? Or did it push up against an even greater counterforce? This is the question we all must ask when the focus of sinking our "Relation-Ship" becomes the operant power.

I have the dearest of friends. I am blessed to have helped them through a difficult and traumatic time in their relationship. This is only my experience with them. I do not claim to be a counselor or therapist of the traditional kind. My advice came from a place deep inside my heart and soul that was not of my mental doing. Once I opened up, out of love and compassion to their pain, infinite wisdom and knowing flooded in. The lessons I learned simply by being of service to them, changed my marriage and relationships forever. I will not recede into the old habits and erroneous reacting of the former me. Now I know, as I am known.

We will call our couple Mary and Joe. This beautiful pair was the envy of most that knew them; they were attractive, full of passion for life, and synonymous with a Hollywood romance. These two were engrossed in doing what they enjoyed and wanted together. A child did not fit into their ambitions. One day, they both had the same epiphany. After years of being married, they wanted a baby more than anything in the world. These two love birds were blessed with a gorgeous baby boy. They were all so in love and content with the abundance life was rewarding them with. After the baby was about four months old, Mary wanted to focus on getting back in shape and lose the baby weight she had gained. She was a gifted athlete with a fit body before she got pregnant. Running became the vehicle for her return to fitness. She would get up early and run with a local group. This energetic gang encouraged each other to compete in foot races. The training continued and fitness turned into fanaticism. Running became a dominate force in Mary's life.

As the months ticked by, this crew grew very close. Late night partying together was a common occurrence. Mary started to shun her husband and child. She was spending more and more time away training, competing, and raging with her new friends. Eventually, Mary made an adulterous mistake. She cheated on her husband with a member of the running group. Joe found out by "accident" from a mutual friend of theirs. He was devastated. He even went to the weekly gathering of her group and denounced them, exclaiming Mary would not be returning. With Joe being a dear friend of mine, my heart was breaking for this incredible family. I knew I had to help and give some kind of support and advice. His constant lamenting and sadness was an anchor pulling them all down. The kicker here is Mary would not stop training with and seeing the running crew. She was obsessed and her ego was writing checks her marriage could not cash.

Meanwhile, one of my best friends told me about an incredible book he was reading, *Zero Limits* by Dr. Joe Vitale. I read the book and learned the techniques he revealed in his text. He tells of a Hawaiian doctor who was head of the state mental hospital. Challenged by the number of hopeless patients, he used a secret ancient Hawaiian practice called "Ho'oponopono" to heal the lost and sick. Each day he would stay in his office and read the charts of the patients. These were mentally sick criminals that were too deranged to be in a traditional jail. As he read their files, he would pray over them in the following manner, "Please forgive me, I am sorry, thank you, I love you."

This wise doctor was enlightened via a sacred teacher on the island. He believed that he attracted these inmates and patients into his life. It was his responsibility through the position he held to heal them. He personally took in each individual. Day after day, he meditated on the inmates, never physically meeting with any of them. He would see them acting out and having to be restrained due to crazy episodes. No attention was ever paid to these events. The nursing staff was becoming irritated by their new director and losing hope. Yet, as the doctor persisted with what he called, "cleaning his energy," the inmates started to change. Daily altercations began to decrease. Drugs and restraints were on the decline. The staff had no idea what was happening. Eventually, all the patients were transferred to a normal jail or prison and the hospital was shut down.

I was shocked the first time I read this story. It just seemed impossible! Later in the book, it is revealed that a few members of the staff were interviewed and confirmed the events at the hospital. The "cleaning" process the doctor described was the key to this miracle. He explained that we are all made up of energy; we attract into our lives that like energy via the universal Law of Attraction. Hence, when you have a negative point of attraction and want to clear the connection, it needs to be "cleaned." By taking responsibility for what you have attracted and not giving resistance to it, then stating over and over again many times a day as you visualize and meditate on the malady, "please forgive me; I am sorry; thank you; I love you," you begin to clean that connection to the person in your life. You take full responsibility for the events and circumstances that that person represents directly to you.

My attention and focus went squarely to Joe and Mary. I thought that this precise technique could be the saving grace for their sinking "Relation-Ship". I explained the basics of the Ho'oponopono cleaning process. Then, I handed Joe the book and asked him to suspend his disbelief. "Read this book as if you were in a movie theater watching it play out," I told him. He did exactly that and personally connected with the amazing claims of the book. Joe was a spiritual person with a strong affinity for the unknown. I was encouraged by the potential for his adoption. Leaving him alone for awhile, with no calls or contact, I knew he would have to be the one to change his marriage. My hope was that he could see this was part of his doing. He was distraught and retreated right to the offensive when I told him that he was partially responsible for Mary's cheating. I believed in the Ho'oponopono cleaning and fully embraced it before I presented it to Joe.

Eventually, Joe was ready to try this ancient technique. He called me about a month after completing his third reading of the book. By this time, out of frustration and hurt, he went to Mary's parents and told them to talk some sense into her. They were too afraid to confront her and just buried their heads in the sand. I can still hear the quivering tear-soaked voice of Joe, as he told me he was ready to divorce Mary. My instincts abruptly interrupted his breaking point speech and said, "Then you have nothing to lose." We talked about how this Hawaiian practice would change his energy and therefore change Mary's point of attraction to him. Then the Marcus Aurelius (121-180), Emperor of Rome, quotation popped in my head. Joe loved historical aphorisms, so I knew this would help his awakening, "Accept whatever comes to you woven in the pattern of your destiny, for what could more aptly suit your needs." He was ready to release his feelings of pain and victimization. His young son was the driving force in his decision. Joe was from a divorced family and could not imagine dragging their boy through that chaos and disorder.

"Mary is my soul-mate Billy." Joe proclaimed. His love was deep for his family. I was amazed by his dedication and conviction to his wife. Most people have such an overcompensated ego, they would give up on the marriage. We human beings want to feel love at the core. This is the most powerful force in the universe. In spite of that, people give up out of the pain and rebellion instinctively. I was hopefully inspired by Joe. He was committed and nothing was going to take his family down. We talked on the phone and in-person for the next couple of months. Most conversations were filled with his Ho'oponopono cleaning sessions details. His conviction to this process was remarkable. He would watch his wife leave for the night, knowing she was going out to the clubs with the very friends that were party to her demise. Offering up no resistance, he would with peace and love repeat many times a day, "Please forgive me, I am sorry, thank you, I love you." Imagining Mary changing her ways and choosing her family over the erroneous activities was his Ho'oponopono healing.

Joe never lost faith or hope, even though day after day, night after night, he was challenged by his thinking mind. His new belief in the Ho'oponopono technique was like a pit bull locked on to it. Reading *Zero Limits* was the tipping point for the new decisions he made to focus on what he could change. Before, understanding the point of attraction, Joe would argue with Mary and give her ultimatums and threats if she did not change. The childhood Mary experienced was wrought with abuse and struggle. This was partially why Joe was patient with her. She would play out reactionary scenes that related to past abuse and rebel against any one trying to control her. At one point, Mary even turned on me. Her pain was so deep that she began to live her life looking in the rear-view mirror. When I told her that, she was infuriated with me. I felt like I was a close enough friend to chime in. She completely disconnected from me after that exchange.

My doubts were starting to surface as time went by. Joe disconnected from me as well. Mary was not going to be controlled by two men teaming up on her. I just prayed for them and let go and let God. Then the most incredible thing happened. One day Joe asked to meet with me. As we talked, I noticed this crystal clear light in his eyes. His face was glowing. His energy was light and bright. Joy was just flowing out of him like lava. Mary slowly and consistently came back to him, he said. She began to stay home and chose her family over other activity. Her love filled their home again and she and Joe reconnected on a level they had never known before. Joe decided not to mention the Ho'oponopono process to her. Once he completely cleaned his energy of resentment, hate, fear, and judgement, everything he attracted changed. The final quotation I gave him was from Dr. Wayne Dyer, one of his best, "When you change the way you look at things, the things you look at change."

This story remains the most transformational and unlikely relationship tale of reversal I have ever encountered. My buddy's marriage, by all marital statistics, should have sunk or crashed against the rocky shore of the world. It always surprises me, how many of us choose to remain focused on what we do not want. Out of instinct and horrible habits, the anchor of repetitious relationship behaviors pull us down. People need to be first it seems. The general concept of being of service to the other person seems to get lost over time. I reiterate, I believe success leaves clues. If you want to take a quantum leap in experience just find someone that is getting the results you seek. When I meet a couple that has been married for twenty years or more, I ask them what the secret to their success is. I must have asked over one hundred couples to date. However, after all the wonderful expressions of faith, hope, patience, comedy, and love, the following one is my favorite.

One day my wife and I attended a benefit, supporting abused children. (I enjoy offering up my DJ-ing services to special causes). We were "coincidentally" seated at the same table with the president of the organization. She had served this community for the past thirty years helping abused children deal with what their lives' situation had given them. Her kind and pleasant demeanor was cherubic. She was joined by her husband of forty years! Of course, this was the perfect couple to ask my best-loved question to. And to date, it is still the most lasting advice I have received. "We do not keep score," she said. More to the point, her explanation was brilliant. "I will do the dishes and put them away. I do not then expect him to clean the house to even the score. If he washes the car, he does not expect me to do the grocery shopping." This is the relationship art of being of service, always! When you put the other person's needs and desires before yours, you have opened the connecting link via service. The Law of Identical Harvest kicks in and the positive flow of energy is returned to you in kind. This is the great practice to all successful "Real-lation-Ships."

In contrast to this wise tenet, I have seen the opposite displayed more often than not. A wonderful couple I know has fallen into the trap of, "being in the world." How many relationships are bombarded by the effects of the physical world? The Joneses tend to be the perfect example of a relationship lost at sea and sinking! Too often couples become overwhelmed with the need to compete and stand out in the world. This couple was sunk with materialism or as my daughter puts it, "stuff sick." When times are good, they are rolling in it. If money becomes tight and they cannot buy the status that is linked to their identity, depression and conflict ensues. The material wealth they had would have been the envy of millions of people. Yet, once they stated to my wife, "We hate our lives; we are so miserable." They are "looking for love in all the wrong places," as the song goes. Tragically, they are searching for identity in the fleeting retail therapy method. "Want is a growing giant whom the coat of have was never large enough to cover." Emerson's words, astutely describe this emotional wreck.

Incredibly, their little dog even became sick. It turns out the cortisol in the dog that is produced by the adrenal glands was shot due to over use. Cortisol is a life sustaining adrenal hormone essential to the maintenance of homeostasis. Called "the stress hormone," cortisol influences, regulates, or modulates many of the changes that occur in the body in response to stress. My hypothesis is that the pet felt the high levels of sustained stress in the home and eventually became exhausted. Animals live in the present moment. If you asked a bird, "what time is it?" if it had a conscious mind to answer, it would say "the time is now." Time is a man-made concept. When animals live with humans and are influenced by them and their emotions, they experience stress and human-like behaviors.

It wasn't until the Joneses focused on giving and being of service to themselves and others that their lives changed for the better. I am amazed by the level of pain and discomfort humans can tolerate. Relationship pain is common and the positions we take because of identity and aimless pride are difficult to shake. Awareness of being is the key to transformation. If you can place that love with yourself before you expect it to come back to you from another, you have just changed your world and the entire world. Once again the sage advice from Emerson rings true, "The remedy of all blunder, the cure of blindness, the cure of crime, is love." How often do we out of reflex and poor habits think of ourself before others? In a society of "you have got to be number one" or "buy this thing to look and feel like a winner" mentality, it is no wonder relationships have declined in effect and longevity.

Living a life based on inertia is no way to live. When times are good and all seems well, you are happy. This is the easiest wave to ride. When life gets rough and that wave attempts to take you under, that is when you can drown. If a relationship is living via inertia, this is the tsunami's forecast. How many millions of couples are out there staying together because of inertia and habit? It is almost like they expect to receive an award for sticking it out.

"We will stay together only for the kids."

"It is too expensive to get divorced."

"How would I find someone to love me?"

"After all, I am too old to date."

"What if I am alone the rest of my life?"

These and many more like it are the statements and dictums of relationship inertia, the recipe for misery and long-held suffering.

What if you started living your relationship life from the end? Inertia could not have an effect on you. What if you started and ended each day imagining what you wanted for the other person over your needs and wants? Coming from a place of, *how may I serve you today*, you are picturing the love and patience you display in your imagination as they return the same to you. You have cleaned your point of attraction via, Ho'oponopono's, "Please forgive me, I am sorry, thank you, I love you." Your whole being throughout this cleaning mantra becomes light and free. It has an incredible power not to be taken for granted. Feelings of forgiveness and peace begin to take you over. No longer do you feel the need to be "the victim" or "the wronged." Your life is this moment here and Now. You come to the realization that time, past and future, are illusions to the thinking mind and all of the negativity done to you is not happening Now. When you really "get it," you move in a direction that is closer than near and sooner than Now. The personal power you gain is transformational and your strength will never leave you again.

I love the Chinese symbol yin and yang. In Chinese philosophy, yin and yang describe how seemingly opposite or contrary forces may actually be complementary, interconnected, and interdependent in the natural world. They give rise to each other as they interrelate to one another. My life has grown with a strong affinity for symbols. Whenever I draw the yin and yang symbol, I feel the balance of oneness that it conveys in shape and design, an equilibrium of energy polarities enclosed in one simple infinite circle. It shows two similar shapes balancing each other perfectly in oneness: one light and one dark. When you live your life as a Now-ist, harmony to all you encounter becomes your natural state of being. Your relationships will become Love "Real-ation-Ships." Your life is always right here, Now-woN!

CHAPTER 13

NOW BECOME A "REAL-STATE" AGENT

---❦---

"The great saint in India, Muktananda, was
asked, 'What is real?' He replied, 'What is real
is that which never changes.' When looking for
what is real and unchanging about ourselves, we
can apply this definition. There is an unchanging
spark from the Creator in each of us, our highest
self, a piece of God. And we are all connected."

— Wayne Dyer

Have you ever thought of someone and how they are feeling, then out of the blue they call you? In 2016, I had a thought about a client with whom I had not seen or heard from in many weeks. I had been the instrument that enabled him to acquire a great windfall of abundance. Working as his property manager, I helped him for six years. Then he wanted to sell his town-home. I attempted to do just that but to no avail. I took the real estate off the market due to the fact that it was over-priced. Months had gone by and a tenant just down the street inquired about places for sale in the immediate neighborhood. I mentioned this town-home and they were hotly interested. After a journey of synchronistic events took place, they bought and closed escrow on the property. This was the buyer's dream unit and they were willing to pay far above the market value. My seller was ecstatic and grateful. He was astonished that anyone would pay that high of a price in the current real estate market.

Long after the deal was complete I thought, *I wonder if 'Tom' really understands just how fortunate he was to sale his property for that price?* I had this feeling at exactly 2:57 p.m. (Yes, I wrote it down.) Then at 2:58 p.m. my phone rang. It was Tom! He was only calling to thank me for the exceptional job I did selling his unit at such a profitable price. Furthermore, he wanted to let me know that he was writing a letter of recommendation about me so others might know the kind of service I gave him. My mind was instantly filled with wonder and amazement. *How is this possible?* Of course, that thought only lasted a minute because I know we are all one and connected. Yet, whenever synchronicity happens, I am soulfully grateful for the experience. It further deepens my faith and inspiration. There are no accidents in this universe of divine order. All is here to serve us and teach us if we are open to the lessons.

What is Real? The revealing words of the thought-provoking Muktananda states, "What is real is that which never changes." It might be difficult for you to wrap your head around this concept. After all, we are in a world that is changing constantly. Our bodies, minds, relationships, and interests change daily. Yet, human beings relate to *real* as solid matter. The dictionary defines *real* as, 1. actually existing as a thing or occurring in fact; not imagined or supposed. 2. (of a substance or thing) not imitation or artificial; genuine. From these two denotations you can see the disconnect in definition and truth. If your body for example is *real*, why can't you find that three year old, little self you were? It existed and had substance with no artificial anything. Was not your teenage self actually here with all its strength and energy? This is the "real" we all look to as the simple truth.

However, when you eventually realize the part of you that IS *real* never changes, you enter the Now. Your focus changes from *Nowhere* to *Now-Here*. It is your imagination that takes you to the most *real* part of your existence. The greatest gift God has ever given us is our own infinite human imagination. The key error in the dictionary's definition of *real* is "a thing not imagined." This can be directly related to the erroneous statement of the French philosopher Descartes, "I think, therefore I am." This 15th Century fundamentalist changed much of the western world with his thought. He related thinking with being and being with thinking. "**I AM**" is the name of God. I am is the very center of being. The obsessive thinking part of existence is most often the key error in realizing true peace and the enJOYment of living.

How can the part of us that is most *real* be accessed by the thinking mind? I relate back to the opening example of my thought about the real estate client. The thought came into my mind. However, the intuitive part of my being, picked up on a connecting link to all sentient beings. We are all **One**. The collective consciousness is accessed not through the thinking mind, but via the dominate power of intuition and imagination. You do not have to try harder to connect to this realm. It is always in the room with you and easily accessed when you let go of thinking. This is how one can have an image, feeling, or idea about one person and the next minute they connect via the timeless Now. It is a journey without distance. This is the natural gifted state of us all. The time-bound world does its work on our thinking mind constantly trying to condition us out of being-ness and deeper into thinking. Yet, "Imagination is more important than knowledge," Albert Einstein declared. He knew Descartes' error and used his power and influence to set the record straight.

The Master Power

Being a real estate agent has given me many examples of what it means to be a *"Real State Agent."* The grand power of this truth always amazes me when I let go and let God. My worldly thoughts can only take me so far on this path of living. Eventually, my imagination will step into the picture and awaken in me the instinctual presence that is *real*. It will appear in life as a super human power that lies dormant until my limited thinking mind reaches its end. Each time it happens in me, I am reminded of a poem by James Allen (1864-1912) which I have committed to memory:

> Mind is the Master power that molds and makes,
> And Man is Mind, and evermore he takes
> The tool of Thought, and, shaping what he wills,
> Brings forth a thousand joys, a thousand ills:
> He thinks in secret, and it comes to pass:
> Environment is but his looking-glass.

I remember a rental that I managed which had remained vacant for too long. The owner was getting impatient. It seemed the more time that went by, the stronger the fearful and negative feelings grew. Doubt began to sink its teeth into my being and ability, which in turn forced me into the present moment's power. Once I reached the limit of "Doing," my "Being" stepped in and changed my stars. It occurred to me, the only reason the rental property had not been filled was due to the fact that I had not placed a tenant in it. Yes, the landlord of the property saw the lack of occupancy and focused on that. I made the choice to go to my most powerful human imagination and place the tenant.

My imagination and Now-ist presence hovered high above planet earth and marveled at the gorgeous, heavenly body we all call home. From that vantage point, I looked down at the vacant property and saw a middle-aged couple living in the house. He had salt and pepper colored hair and hers was brown. They were filled with such joy simply being in this home that it reached me as I gazed down on them. I felt the spirit of Christmas as they celebrated in their new home with their family. Love seeped out of the living areas and made all there, richer and fuller. Next, came the various birthday parties and wonderful family meals at the dinner table. As the grand children came over for a visit, the home swelled with even more joy and abundant love. I engaged all five of my senses in imagination. I could smell the turkey dinner at Thanksgiving. My heart felt the love as the family prayed at the dinner table. I almost tasted the home-made bread the grandmother was baking. Finally, I heard the laughter and music that is family. For family is love in a bunch.

This experience of imagination was exactly what I repeated for seven days straight right before I would go to bed and first thing in the morning. I ran this mental-movie in my mind and felt it in my heart. On the eighth day, a call came in for a couple of the very description that I imagined in my mental-movie. When I met them at the showing my heart jumped. There they were! The very couple I imagined in the flesh! As they introduced themselves and told me about their family make-up, I felt like I could have filled in the application for them. They had grown children and grandkids and loved having family over. They absolutely wanted this home which fulfilled all their needs and desires.

The inspiration is always there in our hearts and minds. This family was destined for this property. They put their intention out into the universe. My choice to let go and let God connected the link. My imagination and instinctual presence was the catalyst for change. The tenant materializes when you think from the end, instead of about the end. You go to that end with all five of your senses fully engaged. You give the images all the tones and feelings of reality. We always attract into our lives, not what we want, but only what we are.

Give to Live

The most amazing things happen in your life when you learn that the key to living is giving. The *Give to Live* mantra has always been the key focus in my life. From a very early age, I was taught that is it more blessed to give than to receive, as it states in the bible. This spiritual hunger that is the driving force in my life is sparked when I am of service to others. It is the match that ignites the light of the world inside each and every one of us.

One night, I watched the wonderful life story of Saint Mother Teresa. She answered that call inside her heart to be of service to the most poor and impoverished human beings in the world. She was the prime example of humility and service to us all. She never wanted credit or acclaim for her work and good deeds. She vehemently stuck to her vows as a nun. She literally changed the world with her example of service. Her most humble acceptance speech for the Noble Peace Prize in 1979 further shined the light on world-wide poverty and she became a symbol of service.

Mother Teresa was canonized as Saint Teresa of Calcutta on September 4th, 2016. This slightly-built giant of a soul was the prime example of what it means to be of service to others. Her intention was simple and pure. Thoughts of *what is in it for me* never even entered her mind. Yet, the point of attraction she emitted from the Holy Spirit changed the world forever. Jesus tells us in Luke 6:38, "Give, and it will be given to you. A good measure, pressed down, shaken together and running over, will be poured into your lap. For with the measure you use, it will be measured to you." This is how you become a Real State Agent. You must give without any thoughts or feeling of giving in hopes of getting. When you truly understand this way of being, your whole life with change forever. Once you learn to *Give to Live*, your old way of living will seem like some other life.

My heart has always been rooted in service. I am not telling you this to seem altruistic. My intention is to teach and inspire you in hopes that you will adopt a new way of being for your life to be fulfilled and abundant. Recently, I was inspired along with my band mate to create a benefit concert and give the proceeds to a worthy cause. It was winter and the weather was increasingly getting colder. We decided to give one hundred percent of the donations to the Freedom Warming Center of Santa Barbara. This wonderful organization gives the homeless members of our community a dry and safe place to sleep on wet cold nights during the winter. Some of the audience members even brought in coats, blankets, socks, and bedding to donate.

The concert took place in late December. Inspired by the season, the night started with traditional Christmas carols and children sing-alongs. My band, joined with two others, filled the night with the true spirit of Christmas: giving! Music filled the air and warmed the hearts of a full house. When the magical night was over, thousands of dollars had been donated and the countless forgotten-of-the-city were given love and kindness. The spirit of Christmas was alive and well with "Joy to the World" thematically lifting the audience out the door and safely home. A few days later was Christmas Eve. My whole family was excited in anticipation of Santa Claus' visit that night. Before I dropped off to sleep, I checked the email on my iPhone. A message came through from a property management client that lived up north in Canada. She asked me to list their incredible property for sale, instead of for rent. This would more than double the highest priced listing I had ever represented in my ten years as a real estate agent! My heart swelled with gratitude. Instantly my spirit went to Jesus' words of inspiration and guidance, "Give, and it will be given to you. A good measure, pressed down, shaken together and running over, will be poured into your lap. For with the measure you use, it will be measured to you."

I made the connection between the benefit Christmas concert and this blessed email. My heart remembered the passage from 2 Corinthians 9:7, "Each one must give as he has decided in his heart, not reluctantly or under compulsion, for God loves a cheerful giver." Christmas cheer was the inspiration in my heart to give to those less fortunate. My mind was never filled with, *what's in it for me?* Yet, abundance is attracted to abundance. My point of attraction was charged with love and giving. When that is your heart's content, life will begin to *Give* as you *Live*. My hope for you, dear reader, is to make a connection to the inspiration in your heart. Give when you feel inspired. No second guessing and rationalizing. Feel the joy that is your gift for the act of kindness. When you resonate at that level of love, abundance is your charged energy field, like energy is coming your way. It is as sure as gravity holding you to the earth or the sun coming up tomorrow.

Imagine if we lived in a world that was solely focused on giving with no thought of return. By virtue of the point of attraction, each individual would generate so much love and abundance, a life of service would be the norm. This is how we can change the world. The Dalai Lama, in his imminent wisdom easily expressed this to the world: "In simple terms, compassion and love can be defined as positive thoughts and feelings that give rise to such essential things in life as hope, courage, determination and inner strength." When you can simplify your focus to this moment Now and come from the place of, "where may I serve?," life will begin to live you. You will become transfigured into a Now-ist.

Fleeting worldly desires will seem more like a game rather than a necessity. In Hinduism, they call this divine game we all live "Lila." Lila is a way of describing all reality, including the cosmos, as the outcome of creative play by the divine absolute. You will have great abundance in all areas of life, although you will not identify with them in some ego driven manner. I am fully aware of the real estate and financial win-fall I acquired via that wonderful email on Christmas Eve. My ego does not have a pay-off amount. My identity is not in the having or the getting. I remain in the giving. When you make this transition from doing to being, the abundance just comes without effort and trying harder. It might seem too easy. You can try and analyze or rationalize, but that is not the way of a Now-ist. Allowing and letting go, this is when your inspiration takes over and intuition and imagination rule your world.

The Real State of your Schedule

Being in the present moment and living like a Now-ist might seem like you need to have an earth-shaking experience or an epiphany. However, the experience and life-style shift is much more subtle than that. As I am in my daily living routine, the schedule that guides and directs my focus has much to do with staying in the present moment. There are days when 15 to 20 appointments and meetings fill my day's calendar. One might think this would cause a great deal of stress. After all, this world of "Doing to Be" seems to be the mantra for the masses. The ordinary person might need a pot of coffee, drink, cigarette, or drug to cope with a day this full. Stress is most people's instant thought and feeling when confronted with an unusually busy schedule. The great teacher Dr. Wayne Dyer forces us to regroup and simplify, "There is no such thing as stress, only people thinking stressful thoughts." If I handed you a bucket and asked you to fill it up with stress, could you find it? This anxiety-provoking thing called "stress" kills more and more people each and every day. Yet, it physically does not exist. According to World Health Organization, the four main causes of death are cardiovascular diseases, cancers, diabetes and chronic lung diseases. Four in every ten deaths worldwide are caused by cardiovascular disease. In terms of proportion of deaths that are due to noncommunicable diseases, high-income countries have the highest proportion – 87% of all deaths were caused by noncommunicable diseases, according to Global Health International Advisors (2012).

The heart is the central feeling organ of the body. When fear, worry, anxiety, and stress take over your physiology, it is no wonder cardiovascular disease is the number one killer in the world. I maintain that a body at *ease* will not create *dis-ease*. Just looking at the day's schedule, jam-packed with commitments and obligations, can generate enough stress for most to reach for their favorite "Escape Pod." This escape usually takes the form of consuming some type of drink, drug, or the like. When that mode of escape reaches its end, they usually have another and another. The mind likes to make up stories and justify this kind of erroneous behavior. After a busy and trying day, it is ok to have a few drinks to unwind. *Everyone does it,* you might think. Yet in the final analysis, heart disease (a heart at *dis-ease*) remains the number one killer year after year.

When I commit to my first scheduled appointment of the day, no other feelings or focus enters my awareness. My attention is fully engaged in what I am doing right here and Now. If a meeting is the current scheduled appointment, my entire energy field and attention is completely there in that engagement. Once that meeting is done, I am on to the next with no lingering thoughts and feelings of the past or worries about future appointments. Stress needs time to exist. Your focus and energy has to live in thought forms with mind-made illusions to create that emotion: stress. Often I remember that old saying about worry and stress if I find myself getting tense or distracted. "Worry is like a rocking chair; it's easy to do but it doesn't get you anywhere." Simple awareness is the key to presence. Energy flows where your focus goes. Practice the art of awareness. Just allow your mind to be where you have scheduled it to be. The quickest method of entering the present moment is to place all of your energy and focus on the breath. I have a transformational practice that keeps me centered and sets me back in balance, should daily living attempt to bring me down.

Breathing into your Heart

The next time you find yourself feeling the stress of daily living, try this: Sit in a chair with your feet on the floor and your spine erect. With your eyes closed, place your right hand in the middle of your chest. Next, put your other hand on top of your right hand. Your palms should be flat, one on top of the other. While holding your heart in your hands, take one deep slow breath. On the inhalation, imagine yourself in your favorite place in the world. It could be on a beach or a mountain top, even a cafe in Italy. My favorite place is hovering above the earth looking at the blue line that encircles our home planet. Now, on the exhalation, feel your senses engage in that place you have imagined. I for one, feel the warmth of the sun as it crests the earth. My senses all relax as I am awe-struck by the majesty of the planet. On the second inhalation, your hands remain on your heart, as you breathe in the gratitude for all you have in this moment. It is very important to focus on just one feeling of gratitude. For example, I am thankful for the ability to hug a loved one. My heart is pressed up against their heart further deepening the connection of oneness. I feel my arms wrap around them and melt in the warmth of the loving embrace. The exhalation this time is filled with the feelings of that gratitude. My heart is feeling the physical presence of my loved one and I am fully engaged in that hug. Keep in mind that your breath is very deep and your exhale is to be slow in rhythm. The third and final breath takes place back at your favorite place in the world. This inhalation sees the images of your location with even more clarity and vividness than the first breath. You notice a deeper color scheme to the sights. More detail is presented to your vision. The last exhalation is filled with your favorite sounds or music. I sometimes hear the low sustained sound of the earth with all of its energy and power, accompanied by a chord of strings blending in nicely. The energy of the music is so wonderful that it takes you along with it as you free yourself from all the stress you were feeling before you breathed into your heart.

Breathing into your Heart

Breath one: *Inhalation-* Imagine seeing yourself at your favorite place.

Exhalation- Feel your senses while being in that space.

Breath two: *Inhalation-* Breathe in the gratitude in the moment for one thing.

Exhalation- Feel the energy and emotions of that gratitude.

Breath three: *Inhalation-* See with even deeper clarity your favorite place.

Exhalation- Hear your favorite sounds and music.

This is the key to choosing the best for yourself, instead of reaching for that escape from so-called reality. If you can practice breathing into your heart and create a new healthy habit of consistently coming back to the Now, your life will never be the same. Feeling good is feeling God. When you realize you are God, your choices will support the most powerful presence that is you. Life will live you and the flow of your existence will become the effortless *Being* you really are. Always remember that less is more. When you find yourself doing without awareness of being that is the sure sign balance needs to be restored.

Chapter 14

Detaching from Outcomes: No Goals just Soul

---　❖　---

"By believing passionately in something that still
does not exist, we create it. The nonexistent is
whatever we have not sufficiently desired."

— Nikos Kazantzakis

One day while working at The Oak Tree men's clothing store in
Spokane, Washington, my 17-year-old self was approached by the
owner of the Drezden Modeling agency. She asked me if I had ever modeled
before. I said, "Not really, just a few photographers had encouraged me
to take my picture before." Days later, I was in her photographer's studio
having my first "real" photo shoot. The stars aligned and instantly I was a
professional model. Not long after that shoot, I got my first modeling job.
My agent was excited for me because it was an underwear shoot. This type
of work paid much better than the ordinary clothed advertisements.

Off I went to a dark, industrial building downtown. When I arrived,
two nice ladies met me with light and airy words to soothe my nerves.
They were informed that this was my first modeling job and to go easy
on the greenhorn. Hot lights and very tight "whitey tighty briefs" was the
wardrobe. Being a newbie and very uncomfortable in my underwear, the two
ladies pulled on the briefs to adjust them after every other shot. This did not
quell my anxiety. The entire shoot felt like eight hours, but only lasted two.
Finally, the main photographer told me, "We just need one more shot and

then we are all done." Giggling and holding back the tears, they approached me with a banana. "Can you just put this in the front of your briefs so we can take a picture for my friend? She will get such a kick out it." Completely shocked and numb from the process, I did not know what to say.

Sweating profusely, I did as they instructed, as high-pitched laughter and shrills filled the studio. The professional expensive cameras were instantly replaced with a Polaroid. Flash after flash, the sound of flapping air-dried, Polaroid pictures was intermingled with the girlish giddiness. As I left the studio that night and walked to my car, oddly enough, the feeling of violation was not the dominant emotion. I did feel taken advantage of for certain. However, a powerful over-arching inner sense of new direction practically gave me whiplash from the force of clarity.

I had an unexpected career opportunity that surprised me as much as Christmas morning. Light filled my thoughts and my imagination took off to the "Big Time." My new focus was becoming a professional model. I had a goal that began to take over my thinking mind. Prior to this first "fruity-photo shoot," I was solely intent on attracting a college pole vaulting scholarship. Placing second at the State Championships that year and skipping basketball to train and prepare for my senior year's track season, my energy was split and this was a challenge.

The modeling gigs just kept rolling in and I became very successful, adding television commercials to the resume. Life had given me a budding career at a young age while still continuing to train for my senior year's state track championship. All was progressing nicely when disaster struck like a bolt of lightning. Just a couple months before state, I was competing in an indoor meet at the Kibby Dome in Idaho. Attempting a new personal best, and on my third and final chance to clear the height running as fast as I could, I planted the pole in the box and took off with a powerful lunge. Swinging upside down and preparing to be inverted, the pole snapped! I hit my head on the metal box and cut my arm badly from the shredded fiberglass as the pole broke. My pole vaulting days would never be the same.

Fear consumed my every practice session and meet thereafter. I worked very hard to change my mind and conditioned my body to jump. However, I just would not leave the ground. I had already qualified for the state meet; result, I was going. It just became a matter of mind over disaster. My dad was excited to see me and my brother both competing in the Washington

State High School Track Meet. Brother Gib qualified in the shot put, so this was an all-time high for dad. He even went to the great expense to rent a high quality video camera to film this momentous event. We lived in Spokane and the meet was in Tacoma, five hours away. The pressure was mounting on me and I did not want to disappoint my Pa.

The big day arrived and I was working sedulously to not think about the past, devastating pole-breaking episode. My thoughts were overwhelmed with trying not to think about it, yet that was all I was thinking about. My first attempt was a run-through. My second try was another run-through scratch. My third and final attempt, I was overcome with such fear and doubt that I never even left the ground. Completely gutted and wrecked, I looked at my Pa in the grandstands and just started to cry. He tried to console me, but it was no use. Head hung low, I walked out of the stadium to an empty parking lot and just sat there and cried. Hours passed and I did not move. Still frozen with fear and disappointment, I lost all track of time. This became an anchor that would come to weigh me down for years!

My point in relating these two stories is to illustrate the thinking/conscious mind and the imaginal/subconscious mind. Reverting back to my modeling beginnings, I have one more story that would serve to be the catalyst to my "Imaginations Inauguration." You see, life has a way of giving you signs and plenty of foreshadowing to change. It seems that we spend so much wasted time in step one, which is our initial thought about a desire. Human beings have this innate, almost masochistic ability to choose pain and struggle, when all along, the power is right there within each and everyone of us, our God-given gift to access our higher and resistant-free Self.

Imagination Creates Reality

After my pole vaulting train wreck, I was rather lost and had no defined path to follow. I wish I would have known the now famous words from Dr. Wayne Dyer, "Don't pole vault over mouse turds." Everything has its time, I guess. My father had given me a very powerful book by Norman Vincent Peale (1898-1993) called *The Power of Positive Imaging* when I was just fifteen years old. I read it again and learned about the power of your thinking and imagining. My modeling career had always been consistent and now out of high school, it was time for a change.

Patti, the owner of the modeling agency, labeled me a big fish in a little pond. She said it was time for me to go after the "Big Time" modeling contract. Each year in New York City, the International Modeling and Talent Association (IMTA) held a huge competition to find models. This was Patti's idea for me. She believed in me and thought I had what it takes to "make it" in the Big Apple's modeling biz. The timing could not have been more perfect for me. I was uninspired about my future given that I decided to not go to college because I did not receive a pole vaulting scholarship.

Now, armed with new inspiration and a goal for the first time in months, I began what would come to be my first glimpse into the power of my own manifesting human imagination. Norman Vicente Peale's book inspired this dormant part of my mind: the power of my ability to imagine my reality and attract that image into my life. I learned while reading his book that thoughts are things. If I would just hold an image and believe it, it would appear. He said, "If you can conceive it and believe it, you can achieve it." The very first goal that I set, using my imagination, was to achieve a big time modeling contract.

Peale's goal setting plan is as follows:

Step one: Write down your goals on a sheet of paper numbering each one.
Step two: Post the goal sheet on your bathroom mirror so that you can see them each and every morning.
Step three: Imagine many times each day what those goals look like in reality.

One night as I laid in bed just before I fell asleep, a flash of my goal's image manifested in my imagination. I saw a big ballroom with a sea of tables and people were sitting at them. I looked and saw a big stage with red carpeted stairs leading to it. On the huge screen was a picture of me. I felt so excited just seeing this in my mind that I could not sleep. It had all the tones of reality. This was no dream. This was an actual vision and my new goal-setting practice. Each night before I went to bed and first thing in the morning, I would see this scene play out in my mind. Then I would walk to the bathroom mirror and read my goals out loud as follows:

1. I have a professional modeling contract with a big time agency.
2. I placed in the top ten in the IMTA modeling competition for men.
3. I am of service to others and help whomever I can.

This practice became natural to me. I could not tell the difference from my vision and reality. I was religious and never missed a morning or a night. Throughout the day, it just felt good to hold this image and feel it in my heart and body. As I continued working and preparing for the trip to New York, my belief was strong. I lived it in and walked around as if I were a professional model in New York with a big time contract. This was not ego or arrogance, just great confidence and strength in my inner vision.

My wonderful mentor and instigator of the trip was right by my side the entire long plane trip to the IMTA competition. Dear Patti, this angel of a teacher and mentor, showed me the modeling ropes. She was the spark that started this internal blaze of new direction. Gratitude and trust were the main feelings I held for her throughout the preparation process. I remember clearly looking out the window of the plane flying above New York City. My feelings were those of excitement and adventure. Nothing was going to change my vision for myself. I was ready and conditioned completely in my purpose for going there.

Seven days of competition were intense and rigorously challenging. Runway, editorial photo shoots, commercial acting, high fashion shoots, and many other categories were filled with over two thousand models. Hopefuls from all over the world were in attendance to compete and stake their claim at the biggest competition in the world. It felt like being at the United Nations conference. Many countries were represented and I met the most fascinating people. It made you realize that human beings around the globe all share the same ability to dream and believe in a brighter future for themselves.

After months of preparation and hard work, the big day arrived. I was seated at a table in the most enormous ballroom I had ever seen. Once I collected myself, I looked at the huge stage. It was a deep blood red with red carpeted stairs leading to it. This was just as I imagined it! My childlike amazement was running wild with excitement and enthusiasm. To top it all off, the projection screen that was the back-drop for the stage filled the entire length of the stage. It was gigantic! I must have sat in my chair for ten minutes, catatonic and in awe. This room, this scene, and all were exactly as I had imagined that fateful night in my bed three months ago.

The announcer stepped to the microphone and the evening began with the reading of the results to the week-long competition. Before the winners were revealed, the jumbo screen behind the stage was filled with the picture of the model who placed in the competition. This was so amazing! I felt as if I were in my imagination watching the scene from my bed. It had all the tones of reality because it was reality! My mind was enthralled with the power of belief and positive imaging; I lost track of the results for the competition. When I regained awareness the emcee was announcing 8th place for men's modeling results. Instantly, I got really nervous. *Oh no, I thought.* They only have ten places and my picture has not shown on the screen. That old traitor, doubt, was trying its best to trump my powerful feelings of faith.

Once the 9th place winner was announced, my dear Patti shot me a look that was attempting to be consoling and empathetic. I could feel her loss of belief. Then in that moment, I closed my eyes and took a deep breath. When I opened my eyes the colossal screen was filled with my picture. My table filled with all my fellow competitors erupted with cheers and screams. As I walked up to the stage and one-by-one climbed the stairs, the only feeling in my heart was gratitude. *This must be what it feels like to walk on the moon,* I thought. My feet did not seem to touch the stage as I was looking out on the audience after accepting my award. I completed the loop of my imaginal inspiration to create this reality.

The reason I have shared the two major goal setting events from the early years of my life is to illustrate the power of your imagination and to make this following statement: "I AM not a goal setter any longer." In all heart-felt honestly, I do not believe in writing down goals and setting up a plan to attain them (like I used to). Once I read a book that took you through a series of steps about reverse engineering your goals. It suggested to write down a plan over a period of time with a task-based approach. More over, you look at your goals each day and check assignments off a list to eventually attain this outcome.

Brilliantly, Dr. Wayne Dyer confirmed my feelings and belief about the goal setting process. This one simple and profound quotation condensed all the theories and methods on goal setting down to one single truth: "How could the God of oneness ever recognize twoness?" The first time I read this, it was like a bucket of icy cold water dumped over me. It shocked me into the present moment with such a profound sense of truth; it forever anchored me in that reality. "How could the God of oneness ever recognize twoness!" There it is. The name of God is I AM that I AM. When you write a goal down, you are stating that it exists somewhere in the future. You are charging that goal with doubt every time you look at it and read it out loud or in your head.

When I first learned about goal setting, I wrote them down. I even thought if I wrote down all the steps it would take to accomplish the goal in reverse, I would have a fool proof plan. It was not until I abandoned this practice that the truth was revealed to me. When I was in my thirties, each year on my birthday I would set five or six goals. I loved working on my Mac computer with the list of goals. Using creative fonts and colors to liven up the page that would hold all my hopes for this year's list, I remember the uneasy and restless feeling I got every year setting these goals, not really accomplishing many of the previous year's attempts and having uncertainty as my companion on the entire journey.

Why was this such a hopeful yet hopeless process? I followed all the books and teachers of the time. Each step was there. "If you don't make a plan, you can plan to fail." Quotations like this were intended to scare you into submission and get you busy, I guess. Granted, I did accomplish some of my goals. For those individuals that have no idea about who they "really" are, I understand the methods and terminology for goal setting. I AM talking to you! The YOU that understands I am God. When you say I AM and place an intention with it, that is the power that a step-by-step plan has no relation to. "How could the God of oneness ever recognize twoness?" The quotation at the beginning of this chapter explains the point I am making perfectly. "By believing passionately in something that still does not exist, we create it. The nonexistent is whatever we have not sufficiently desired."

The Power of Imagination Inspiration

When you have a desire, a deep-rooted intention from the truth of your being, all your thoughts break their bonds. The ancient spiritual teacher Patanjali explained this:

> When you are inspired by some great purpose, some extraordinary project, all your thoughts break their bonds: Your mind transcends limitation, your consciousness expands in every direction, and you find yourself in a new, great and wonderful world. Dormant forces, faculties and talents become alive, and you discover yourself to be a greater person by far than you ever dreamed yourself to be.

This is the ultimate power you house within. Most people do not know they have this super power: Inspiration! When you live inspired, you are living In-Spirit. This is the great power known by the prophets, sages and the seers throughout the ages. And that spirit that you are is God. You are the I AM that I AM. How can you be any more powerful than to be a creator? You are the artist of your life. "You can do all things through Christ who strengthens you," as it says in the Bible. When you have this realization, no doubt can ever enter your mind to this fact. Living your daily life becomes a joy when you choose this way of life. I am here to tell you the truth.

You have a super human power. You are more powerful than you have ever known. The power of your own wonderful human imagination is God! The spark of God is the same imagination that created the universe and all there in. Two thousand years ago, Patanjali presented this fact to us from his connection to spirit. He knew this truth and it has always been within each and every one of us since the very beginning. A Now-ist lives in this truth every moment in that illusion of space and time. This is the center of our being, the ultimate illumination of us all. We are omniscient, omnipresent, and omnipotent.

You have this power dormant in you. I liken it to a Super Power because it is similar to Batman, Superman, or Wonder Woman. These everyday people walk around in common hours, do normal jobs and exist in society.

It is only when a challenge or a decision is made by the Super Hero to be extraordinary that the Super Power is displayed. Moreover, we are all born with this power. As little children we know this. Our imagination (which is God) flows freely and is present for the world to see all day long. William Wordsworth reveals this clearly in his *Ode on Intimations of Immortality from Recollections of Early Childhood:*

> Our birth is but a sleep and a forgetting;
> The Soul that rises with us, our life's Star,
> Hath had elsewhere its setting
> And cometh from afar;
> Not in entire forgetfulness,
> But trailing clouds of glory do we come.

This is our very truth and existent hope. I remember spending endless hours in my early years wanting for things and experiences. My identification with social status and keeping up with the "Joneses" was the primary focus of my goals. I always wanted something I could not afford. A goal in my mind was trendy clothing or a new keyboard and the like. Once I was so lost in the wanting and not willing to go through the waiting that I made a huge mistake.

The time was 3 a.m. and I pushed my car down the driveway in order to not wake up the house full of my sleeping family. I was a bell boy at the Ramada Inn near the airport. I had been writing songs on my guitar and really wanted a keyboard to expand my creativity. It would take more than a year for me to save enough to buy such an instrument. My impatience and ego got the best of me. My plan was to sneak into the bar at the hotel and steal the amazing Roland D-50 keyboard that I saw during my shift. The band had recently loaded in their equipment and I basically lost my mind and judgment.

Once I arrived at the hotel parking lot, I slipped into the service entrance near the bar. All the lights were off and I felt my way to the keyboard. I grabbed it and hightailed it out the same door that I entered. Then, I drove home with a sense of malevolence and a sick feeling in my stomach. My engine was off as I coasted down the driveway, only to slink back to my room, carefully trying to not wake up my brother. Covering up the keyboard with blankets, I slid it under my bed and attempted to go back to sleep.

The next day, I was scheduled with the morning shift. I headed into work with trepidation and a lazy sense of disgust. About an hour after, I punched my time card, and a clerk asked me to meet the general manager in his office. *Oh my Lord!* I knew what this was all about. As I walked through the door to his office, the first thing I saw was the police officer and handcuffs. Mr. Valentine, the manager of the hotel, knew what had happened because they had it all on video tape. The officer asked me to put my hands behind my back and proceeded to handcuff me. While reading me my rights, the kind Mr. Valentine said, "Wait a minute. I think I know a better way to handle this crime."

My dad was an acquaintance of his and he knew how much I loved and respected my father. "Here's what I want you to do," he directed. "Officer, please remove the handcuffs. Bill, you are going to bring the keyboard back, and then go to your father and tell him exactly what you have done." Mr. Valentine knew this was a more severe punishment for me, as opposed to, some monetary court fines. You see, dad had fought and sacrificed greatly to get custody of my bother, sister, and me during the nasty divorce years earlier. To disappoint my father was a fate worse than death and he knew it.

I tell you this story to show the human sense of lack we all feel at times. It is not bad to want things or material stuff. We have just collectively lost our sense of identification in the material. I remember not long after my criminal act, I was ashamed of the house we lived in. So much so, that I was at a girl's house and her father offered to drive me home. She was in the car with us. I had her father drop me off at the house down the street. I thought this house looked much newer and therefore by association made me look better. Later, I realized that I was lying. As time teaches, I am thankful for the short-comings in my life. Without them, I would not have known the truth when I discovered it.

The Art of Thinking from the End

Now when inspiration strikes or a manifestation is intended, this is the process of actualization. This is the ultimate power that our creator has placed in each and every one of us: *You must think from the end and not about the end.* In traditional goal setting, you write down what you want to occur. You might even write all the steps you would take to accomplish that outcome. Let's assume you want to attract a love relationship in your life.

You might write down: I want to be in love and in a committed relationship by next year. Ok. You have written down a wish and you look at that goal each and everyday as many millions of people do. You take action and promise yourself that you will enter dating sites, go to dinner parties, and put yourself out there. You look at the empty space next to you in bed and feel lonely. Day after day passes by and the mate you want so desperately in your life seems to be far, far away.

You have not thought from the end, only about the end. How could the God of Oneness ever recognize Twoness? How can the almighty power that creates worlds ever know lack or scarcity. The person setting this goal might even pray vehemently on their knees every night in tears of sadness. "Please dear God, send me a soulmate! I am so lonely. I am in great need." Once again, how could a God of Oneness ever recognize Twoness? You are empowering your desire with deep feelings of lack and scarcity. You are precisely pushing away exactly what it is you desire the most.

Here is the process of attracting and manifesting this into your life. Your intention is to attract a love relationship. Now you go to the end. You imagine with all the tones of reality, the hair, the eyes, and skin color of your dream person. You see how the light catches their figure. The clothing is so vivid to you it is almost like you are watching a movie in high definition. The sound of your loved one's voice is so clear that you know your name is meant to come out of their mouth. You feel the embrace and you are no longer two individuals, but one. When you smell the pheromones of your lover, peace washes over you. You kiss your dream person. The vision is complete and all is happening right here and NOW!

Each day you awake and every night before you go to bed, you play this movie in your movie-mind. You enhance it with all five of the senses. You do this not in the future. This is all happening now. You are thinking from the end, not about the end. This is not a goal. This is reality. You go to your wonderful human imagination and believe it in. When you come back to this moment, you should feel as if you cannot imagine your life without this person. It is so real that time has no affect on this intention. You then find some way to be of service to someone that is in need of what you desire. You pay it forward and expect nothing in return. "Give, and it will be given to you. A good measure, pressed down, shaken together and running over, will be poured into your lap. For with the measure you use, it will be measured to you" (Luke 6:38).

CHAPTER 15

YOU NEED TO DIE BEFORE YOU DIE

---❧---

"Death is the best thing in life. There is nothing in life
like death, but people take such a long time in dying. At
least, their neighbors never see them rise from the grave."

— William Blake

What are our greatest fears? I am quite certain that if you polled one million people on this planet, you would find death at the top of the list. It is not so much that we spend our waking hours upright and solely focused on this fear. It is the movie score that is playing very low and distant in the background of your "Movie Mind." I full-heartedly love going to the movies. Most days, music is constantly playing in my mind and heart for whatever is manifesting in my life. If I am playing with my daughter, a sweet string section fills the moment. (In all honesty, I actually hear this music audibly in my head). When my wife and I are in a deep intimate moment, Marvin Gaye will start to play, "Let's Get It On." Winning a golf tournament, walking up the 18th hole, the Rocky theme will instantly ring out in my ears. Ultimately, a challenge of some kind will enter my awareness. "The Eye of the Tiger" by Survivor will hit hard with the guitars and crash symbols rocking my inner world.

This is my own score to my own life. Daily, the songs and instruments change. I am a musician. Music is a huge part of what makes me up. Sometimes throughout the day, inspiration will strike me and an original song is born. The mood can create whatever my attention is consistently focused on. Being a Now-ist and a musician creates the best symbiotic relationship for manifestation. Emotions that are conveyed in a song or a piece of music universally touch the planet and elevate the energy of the being. Music, as it has been stated many many times, is the one universal language. To create pure music, one must connect to the infinite source of creativity and enter that state of detachment from the worldly grip. You do not have to be a musician, poet, painter, writer, or performer to be an artist. We are all artists. The very definition of *creation* is the action or process of bringing something into existence, or a thing that has been made or invented, especially something showing artistic talent. The dictionary further defines creation as, the bringing into existence of the universe, especially when regarded as an act of God.

In Romans 4:17 we are told, "God calls things that are not seen as though they were seen, and then the unseen becomes seen." This pure description of the process and promise of your most powerful human imagination is the key and greatest of all the secrets in the bible. No other force in our mortal existence is creating so rapidly and remains unchecked and uncontrolled by billions of people. The masses are filled with fears, worries, stress, anxiety, doubt, and depression. Images in the media, television, and newspapers all scream at us daily, in the bleeding and leading, headline stories. They have the populations right where they want them. STRESSED OUT! Unable to relax and wondering why they have such a difficult time falling asleep after that nightly dose of misery. Of course, right after the nightly news, sleeping pills and many other malady type drugs are endlessly pitched to soothe the weary viewer. Imagine what these types of people feel in their bodies and picture in their minds. They do not make the connection with the God-given power of imagination-manifestation and the negative outcomes constantly created in their own lives.

You have to die to your former self. You have to die to the old ideas and imagining the cancers of the mind. One has to die to the past and future every moment. Anxiety has no positive creative power. One's lack of presence will dig that worldly grave faster than a pill or drug can react to the physical body. William Blake speaks to this point perfectly in this poignant observation, "Why stand we here trembling around calling on God for help and not ourselves in whom God dwells." New ideas can only spring into life with fresh starts and our awareness of consistently focusing our attention on the highest and best outcomes. A seed has to die and be buried in the ground before it can be made alive and bear fruit. Death has nothing to do with the physical body, we never die anyway. There is always an opening and an expansion of self. In your mind, you have to see yourself and your destructive ways being buried and give thanks. You have to die to your former ideas so that new ideas may take root and form.

Jesus died on the cross so that the lower form of the human body can be transformed into the heavenly body of enlightened oneness in divine perfection. He was abused, beaten, bloody and broken. This is the letting go you have to take on to die to the past and future in the only power you have to transform your life: the Now! You shed the lower-self to gain the higher-self. Once you have freedom from the worldly focus of materialism, the presence of the Now is all that you are. The Now-ist will never return to the false-self of the world. Crucifixion comes before resurrection. Crucifixion without resurrection would be completely unthinkable; "My God! My God! Why hast thou forsaken me?" You get lost in the beginning of this transformation. You want to hold fast to the world and the problems you have grown numb to and exchanged for identification. For most it is scary to change. Yet, we are to be in this world, not of this world, as Jesus inspires us to change.

The Fearsome Five

How do you focus your most heart-felt states of being daily? Is your day filled with stress? Do you stop every once in a while and think, *What am I doing in this job, relationship, conversation, or negative undertow?* You might find yourself thinking and feeling at the same time, conflicted by what your mind tells you and your heart feels. This is the daily battle in the hearts and minds of the masses globally. Why else do we see drug and alcohol use at an all time "high?" The average human being does not make the connection to the common inertia-based feeling in their body, ignited by their thinking mind. A rough start to the day could look like the following:

A power outage hits at home. Your alarm clock does not go off as usual. Rushing to get ready for work, you snag your shirt on the door jam and rip it. Hurrying even more, you wipe toothpaste on your pants. Out the front door and driving your car, you run into the corner of the garbage can in your driveway and dent the fender. Traffic is making you even later, although you missed the morning rush hour. Finally, you make it to work and all the thoughts and scenarios you were running in your head about being late to work materialize, just how you worried them into existence. The truth is you probably should have turned around and went back to bed!

The inertia you created by all the stress, worry, fear, and anxiety was more powerful than Niagara Falls. Momentum, inertia, focus, and the power of your energy create your reality. The stacking affect of your emotions can drag you along the roaring rapids of life. Your "Movie Mind" scored your entire morning to nerve-grinding, intense music with images of car crashes and breaking glass. If you were to check in with your body during this morning from hell, your shoulders would be rock tight with facial expressions cutting into every line on your face. To break this insane pattern, you need to rock the very core of your center and crush the mind-made-movies you continually play when life sends you into the rapids. You must remain aware and deeply present in the Now to turn that river into Lake Placid.

Our sweet daughter screamed out one night. She was almost asleep when she had the most terrifying, lucid nightmare. I rushed to see what was the matter and she was in the fetal position, eyes open, crying and breathing fast and furious. No matter what I said or did, I could not calm her down. She would not respond. First, I tried to remind her what I taught her about fear. It is only F, E, A, R. Fart-Evidence-Appearing-Real. This seemed to break through a little bit. Then in that moment, I came up with the Fearsome Five!

1. Lay on the bed how you would if you were totally relaxed and feeling peaceful and calm.
2. Breathe how you would breathe if you were completely full of peace and joy.
3. Close your eyes and imagine a scene from a movie that makes you feel great and happy.
4. Smell what you would smell if you were eating your most favorite goodies.
5. Feel with your heart the love and warmth you feel from the most special person in your life.

Once she did all five of these, she was completely at peace and fell asleep. The next morning, I asked her about the previous night. She was very vague and could barely remember the scary and overwhelming event.

Our brains mostly want to avoid pain and gain pleasure. Children know this instinctively and do not over-think it. I did not press my dear one on this initially upsetting event, because I knew that to think feelingly of the past just reinfects the mind and body. The power of the Fearsome Five was shocking to me in that moment. I was amazed by how fast it worked on her fear. Only a few minutes had passed from total terror and hysteria to peace and relaxation. The universal power of the Now has infinite benefits. When one can connect whole-heartedly with the grand power of the present moment nothing is impossible to you. Life will become simple when you learn the daily practice of being a Now-ist. Showing my daughter how to focus her imagination in a crisis moment empowered her to learn in real-time, just how quickly the Now can give clarity.

She did not hesitate. Listening to my calm voice and trusting me in concert with her own human imagination, she entered the state of the Now-ist. She became an alchemist, transforming base metal into gold. Albert Einstein's famous advice was my final thought as I tucked my little angel into bed that night, "If you want your children to be intelligent, read them fairy tales. If you want them to be more intelligent, read them more fairy tales." Imagination is the greatest gift God has ever given us. It is now up to us to use this golden truth to fill our hearts and lives with all the wonder and fulfilled dreams we can imagine in that child-like bewilderment.

The Now-ist 9

When I look at my life, and the current state of my being, day-in and day-out, my humble heart is filled with such joy and gratitude to the great ones that have inspired this change at my soul's core. I have always had an intense spiritual hunger. I have never truly understood why, until the calling to write this book was powerfully revealed to me. When I finally learned how to get out of my own way and just "Let go and let God," as they say in the recovery movement, all was presented and present to me and my awareness of being. When I completely understood the I AM presence, which is the all-encompassing Now-ist truth, all became crystal clear.

Having a deep conversation with Pa one day, he reminded me of a powerful life-changing moment we shared together when I was just leaving high school. He said the "nest" is where the real life training happens as it relates to the parent-child relationship. The love, support, and confidence you gain stays with you as you prepare to leave the nest. The values and challenges, disappointments and victories you experience, have the safety and comfort in the context of the nest. You have a support network of love and family to fall back on. Life's wins are sweeter when shared with those you love and love you. The nest is paramount in filling you with the love and direction you need to leave the nest and go your own way. Listening to Pa's smooth and sagacious voice always sets me right in heart and in mind.

The nest is the key for transforming you into the Now-ist presence and the catalyst for this most important shift in your awareness of being. I am fully aware of many readers' challenging familial experiences. The nest probably did not even exist in its truth for you. Most families have a dysfunction and are riddled with deep-seeded pains and memories with ghosts that never seem to leave your mind. The past is constantly scratching to get back to your present thoughts and feelings. For you, I find this nest to be a new and fresh home. The nest is the Now-ist Nine's home. The best way to experience this is as its own home in you. This is your NEST. **N**ow-ist **E**ssential **S**trength **T**raining:

1. **I AM that I AM** is the name of God which is also YOU. When you finally come to the realization and full acceptance of this long forgotten truth, your life will never be the same.

2. **Imagination** is the greatest gift you have ever been given. *I'm* is the contraction of *I Am*. I'm-Imagination. *I* and *M* are the first two letters of *imagination*. I am imagination is the name of God. When you use your imagination, you are using the power of God. That is the I AM presence that is your birth right and ultimate truth.

3. **Inspiration** or another way to say it is "In Spirit." I walk in the spirit ninety percent of the day. I am always coming back to the present moment when life attempts to distract me with problems, challenges, or wrong-doings. I look at the world and always want the best for those I come into contact with. Recognizing the connection we all have with one another, we are all from one mind, body and

spirit, coming from the same place and returning to the same place. One-Now-Won.

4. **Thinking from the End** and not about the end. Always imagining your wish fulfilled and completely finished in your imagination. You are not hoping for some goal to happen in the future. You live there in that completed objective fact in the present moment, whole-heartedly and entirely.

5. **Your Concept of Yourself.** Your concept of yourself must support what you ultimately want your life to be. You must focus on what you want, not what you do not want, constantly checking in with your innermost being.

6. **The Law of Identical Harvest.** This universal law rules the world. You must always be aware of it and realize you will only reap what you sow in life. Feeling good and feeling God are the same.

7. **Synchronistic Thinking.** You have the power to control what you attract into your life. Harness this personal power you possess. Live it in, and you will make this habit your new way of life.

8. **Time is an Illusion.** The sages throughout history have all pointed us to this truth. You must completely own this fact and place your attention in the present moment each and every day.

9. **Now-Won.** When you are in the Now you have Won. This is the key to living and attracting all of your God-given power and abundance. When you experience this, you will never be the same.

The Now-ist Nine are essential for your shift in consciousness and rebirth into the knowing you are here and now, always. Your life is lived on a series of levels that consist of varying thoughts, feelings, and emotions. Time is this linear plane of existence. We age, have memories, and place markers in this level of living. Human beings go about their lives and allow this chronological time to rule all aspects of existence. The other dimension of time is rarely paid any attention to. And this is the most powerful and transformative form of time in existence, Divine Time. When you take your linear chronological time and cross it with the awareness and full realization of divine time, in *that moment*, you have entered the *Now!* You have shifted your focus from doing to being. You then find yourself in a new and better world. Patanjanli says it best, "When you are inspired by some great purpose, some extraordinary project, all your thoughts break their bonds: Your mind transcends limitations, your consciousness expands in every direction, and you find yourself in a new, great and wonderful world. Dormant forces, faculties and talents become alive, and you discover yourself to be a greater person by far than you ever dreamed yourself to be."

I would now like to take you deeper into each one of the Now-ist Nine.

1. **I AM that I AM.** Say it just as it is written. Do not attempt to think or wrap your head around it. "I am that, I am." This is the name of God given to Moses on the mountain. God's one and only name for all generations forever and ever. This is the only place in the entire bible that God's name is given. I am that, I am. Imagining God is telling Moses *that*, and he is referring to *that* bush God is in. Then imagine God is pointing to *that* mountain over there. Imagine *that* sky above Moses' head. God is in everything and everyone throughout the entire universe. Now say it again. I am *that*, I am. Do you feel the truth? Can you become one with *that* feeling of God that is, I am *that* I am? It is not blasphemous to say, I am God. Paul says in Philippians 2:5-6, "Let this mind be in you, which was in Christ Jesus: Who, being in the form of God, thought it not robbery to be equal with God."

2. **Imagination** is the power to change your life as fast as a lighting bolt strikes the earth. God-the-universe likes speed. Imagination begins with the trust in the image you instantly focus on and power it with feeling. You picture it in your being. Your faith in the feeling and engagement of all your senses create the reality in your life. You imagine from the end as a fulfilled event, as if you were watching it on the movie screen completed and whole. It has all the life of reality in your imagination. You go to the end with full commitment in the Now. Your attention is focused and every part of your being is present in that actualized outcome. You always enter the picture in the Now. Imagination always has to have the feeling senses to fuel the vibrational alignment with the objective fact.

3. **Inspiration** is the blood of the soul. When you live in spirit whole-heartedly with abandon of mind-made limitations, you have crossed over to the other shore. Life is your dream to live. You become an attractor to all that is good and true. People are magically drawn to you. When you give your heart, time, talent, treasure, and love with no need for return, that is inspiration. You become a magnet to the abundance your soul and spirt actualize. The Now is the spirit's home and resting place. When you are inspired you become one with the energy that created you. You are like imagination spreading out to the whole world when you are inspired. Your field of energy reaches others on the same level of connection and oneness.

4. **Thinking from the End** and not about the end. Here your imagination is engaged with all five of your senses present in your fulfilled wish. You see exactly what it is to be here and now with no time, just present objective fact of actuality in your imagination. You need to close your eyes and see the outcome with all the tones of reality. When you become fully committed to this practice, your manifestations will become the legends of your life. Most people pray to God for help or deliverance of something. This prayer comes from scarcity and lack. You must always pray with gratitude and thanksgiving of your wish already fulfilled. After all, how could the God of one-ness ever recognize two-ness? The almighty would not exist. Two-ness requires a split, for there can only be One-Now-WON!

5. **Your Concept of Yourself** is what you walk around with each and every day. Is your concept focused on what you want or what you do not want? The vast majority of the population has a terrible habit of worrying and staying in a negative focus. You must control this inner voice that is endlessly filling your head with a story that does not support what you want. Why is there so much struggle and strife in today's world? I'll bet if you could broadcast the thoughts and inner dialogue of people walking down the street, an overwhelming majority would be negative. Make this connection and make a quick correction to the good.

6. **The Law of Identical Harvest** states that like is attracted to like. You reap what you sow in other words. Catch yourself when you start that old habit or pattern of negative focus. You get what you think about all day long, whether you like it or not. Why not recognize this truth and manifest with conscious positive focus! This universal law is equal with gravity, relativity, inertia, and so on. Why not harness this power with your own present moment awareness and finally realize, thoughts are things!

7. **Synchronistic Thinking** is your power to create your world on a super human level. When you realize that you can manifest from your thoughts, you feel like you are a real-life-magician. You must begin now to make the connection to your conscious thoughts and your God-given ability to manifest. There are no accidents in the universe. All has its purpose. All of creation is complete. It is simply a matter of your joining that outcome in the material world to bring it to fruition.

8. **Time is an Illusion** of human invention and erroneous obsession. The greatest thinkers have all proved this truth. Yet, most everyone spends unnecessary energy and focus on this myth. Of course, we all have to keep calendars and schedules for appointments and special moments in time. That is all fine and well. The drama and pain occurs when you identify your being-ness with time. Once you completely understand the only way out of time and into peace is the Now, you will then "Time Travel" from NO-where to NOW-here.

9. **Now-Won** is the discovery through the anagram Now-Won, that when you are in the Now you have Won. Has there ever been a time or event that happened to you in any other moment than now? The now is all you have and all you ever will have. When you realize this and fully make it your truth, recognizing the profundity, peace and joy become your Now. Everything else is just the mind's mental dance. The present moment is the joy and peace that takes you out of stress and delivers you freedom. In one single moment of presence and detachment from outcome or identification with objects in time and space, you are present NOW!

I am here to be of service to all. It is my ultimate calling to share this wisdom that has chosen me. I am in alignment with this truth and my nature is to give. "For it is in giving that we receive," as the Prayer of Saint Francis inspires us all to action. *WE* are truly all *ONE*. When you can make this omnipotent realization the foundation of your shift, then, the *NOW-WON* transformation becomes a natural evolution of your divine presence and being.

CHAPTER 16

CLOSER THAN NEAR AND SOONER THAN NOW

"Your mind does not know the way, our heart has already
been there, and our soul never left… welcome home."

— Emmanuel

The movie *Taken* is a popular story about an ex-mercenary whose daughter is taken while traveling with a friend in Paris. His speech while talking to the captor on the phone has become legendary, *I don't know who you are. I don't know what you want. If you are looking for ransom I can tell you I don't have money, but what I do have is a very particular set of skills. Skills I have acquired over a very long career. Skills that make me a nightmare for people like you.* - Liam Neeson

This scene in the movie grips the audience and makes you feel connected to the passion in the character's voice. Everyone who ever wished they had a Super Hero type of power relates to this monologue. He is markedly confident and secure in the ability to do whatever it takes to get his daughter back home safe and sound.

The power that lies within you has that same kind of strength and super human ability. What if I told you, you could take a conflict, difficulty, adversary or plain old "bad" situation and be the victor. Your life's situation might be contrary to what you want. Here are a "set of skills" you can learn to conquer any problem or perceived foe you come in contact with. The 13th century Sufi mystic and poet Rumi offers up this inspiration to us all,

"The garden of the world has no limits except in your mind, its presence is more beautiful than the stars, with more clarity than the polished mirror of your Heart." Let us focus our attention on the "garden," the "stars," and the "heart" from the poet. These are all common words or sentiments in the world of art, music, language, and living. They represent something different to us all in a deeper meaning.

The *garden* is a common analogy for the mind. "A man's mind may be likened to a garden, which may be intelligently cultivated or allowed to run wild, but whether cultivated or neglected, it must, and will, bring forth. If no useful seeds are put into it, then an abundance of useless weed seeds will fall therein, and will continue to produce their kind." ~ James Allen, *As a Man Thinketh*

This is the ground where the first skill will be acquired. The mind is the fertile space where all manifestation starts. You must be aware of the mind as a garden, and to always plant what you want and not what you do not want to grow there. You will tend to this garden by remaining focused on the good and plucking out the bad. Your harvest will produce abundance with a simple and singular intent.

The *stars* are the heavenly bodies' light. These ethereal beings of abundance represent power and strength and offer hope to the seer. Here in lies the power of worlds. While we are tending to our garden, we look to the heavens for the light that is our strength to grow. Stars are suns in distant galaxies. The sun allows our gardens plantings to grow. Our wonderful human imagination is that light. We have a thought form in our "garden-mind." We shine the light on the good in our garden. You realize that a weed planted there will grow as fast as the good seed. Our focus and light ray stays only on the image of the fullest harvest of abundance.

The *heart* is the soul of the gardener. This is the center of the universe. If inspiration is the blood of the soul, then the heart is God of the body. When one is clear and present in heart, with only good being the focus and intent, the sweetest and most perfect fruit grows there and a bounty of abundance springs forth. This is the power that creates worlds. God lives in your heart as soul. Here is the presence that is, *Closer than near and sooner than Now.*

When you find yourself becoming stressed, you want to expand your awareness to the most vast presence you are able. The truth that lies in you is infinite and needs immensity to overtake your short-sided thoughts and feelings. Conflict is the point of transformation and the real opportunity to change your stars. Difficult times and challenges are our best teachers. If you can become aware and learn to forecast the signs of hard times or tough luck, you will know that the way out of the erroneous states and negative undertow is to catch it before it takes you down. The soul needs space and immensity. If you can anchor yourself to that vast space that is your soul's natural state of being, life will become a way of living that is *Closer than near and sooner than Now.*

I am Christmas

I am is in word and in being the definition of the power that is *Closer than near and sooner than Now.* When you say **I am**, and know that you are the **I am that I am,** you have entered the Now in its fullest expression. This is the ultimate truth that is omnipotent and omniscient. You will recognize this sooner than Now and closer than near presence when you are a giver. "For it is more blessed to give than to receive," Jesus said. As I write these words it is now Christmas Eve. I am gazing at my family's Christmas tree, feeling all of the magic and joy that is this most wonderful time of the year. This incredible season liberates us to give to those we love and lift humanity to a place it only visits once a year. All who believe, give the joy and peace that is the blessing of the gift-giver.

The story of Jesus' birth creates presence in us, as we contemplate in the knowingness of that incredible miracle of Christmas and the Christmas season. All of the signs and symbols lead us to that one place within, that is Emmanuel, which means God is with us. If the whole world would take a moment and pay attention to the feelings of the Christmas spirit, they would realize God is with them. By a monumental act of reductionism, human beings could finally see that it is in giving that they receive. I can feel the world shift during the Christmas season. For once, the world is focused on giving to others. Charity, faith, hope, love, and well wishes are for those we hold dear. Then after Christmas, attention travels to the New Year and the hope that a fresh start or a new beginning will bring a better life.

Rumi's brilliant poetry shares with the world his insight to the real world. He offers us a system of living that summarizes the process, if you look and read with the eyes of the heart. The final words of his instruction are where I would like you to focus your attention now, "with more clarity than the polished mirror of your Heart." Your heart is the point of attraction to which all that is of like energy and spirit will reflect or become attracted. When you are inspired and moved by the feelings that reside in the center of your universe or heart, all of like feeling and vibration will align with you. You always reflect what you are, not what you want.

When you can make your primary focus, "Polishing the Mirror of your Heart," your life's point of attraction will become love. This is the dominant power that lives in you. This is by definition that power that is *Closer than Near and Sooner than Now.*

The Mirrored Door

So how do you polish your heart? Let go of all trying or doing. Working hard is usually a form of resistance. Awakened doing is what I am talking about here. You have enthusiasm for what you attract into your life. No fear or worry of having to make it happen. You think and feel from the end. You imagine what you want to attract into your life as already here. Your heart is polished when it reflects the exact image the mirror reflects. Your heart is also the haven for feelings. When you match your heart's reflection with the feeling of already being what you want, it will show itself in material form so that you can see what is in the mirror.

How do you experience water? You do not grasp at water and try harder and harder to hold it in your hands. To experience water you become one with it. You immerse yourself into the water and act like water acts, flowing smoothly and softly as it does. You relax into the pure power that forms rivers and streams. All the carving that it has done over millions of years leads back to the greatest body of water, the vast ocean. The Grand Canyon was carved out by a great river over a long, long period of time. Here is a wonderful visual of just how powerful water can be. Time is the illusion that takes our attention away from the force of the waters way of being. The truth is when water is still and placid, it creates its own mirror. When you are like water, the most dominate natural force on the planet will be your example, for reflecting what you most want in your life.

So many human beings look at the polished reflection in their heart's mirror and focus their attention on it. The problem is they are looking at the images in that mirror that occurred in the past and attempt to move forward. Imagine if you were driving down the freeway and only looked in the rear-view mirror. You would not be aware of what is right in front of you Now. Only focusing on what has moved behind you is the sure-fire way to create a devastating crash. Yet, billions of sentient beings live lives with this focus and erroneous behavior. It is no wonder why the wreckage of our fellow travelers is strung-out over the freeway of life for all to witness as we pass by them.

William Blake wrote, "If the doors of perception were cleansed every thing would appear to man as it is, infinite. For man has closed himself up, till he sees all things thru' narrow chinks of his cavern." We cleanse the doors by polishing our perceptions and impressions to such clarity, it is as if it is not there at all. We would then only experience the infinite abundance and power that is, *Closer than near and sooner than Now.* The "doors" could be the opening into the infinite abundance we all seek. Every opportunity would be a further expression of oneness with all that is. Resistance to what is clouds up the door of perception. It becomes dirty and difficult to see the image that is right in front of you.

Before I realized, then actualized this cleansing Blake expressed, my doors of perception were all gray. Continually my perceptions were open to the possibility of the infinite, although my belief was questioning where they led. It was not until I had the *satori*, the flash of enlightenment, that the doors were cleansed once and for all. I was gifted this experience and was blessed to see the infinite from high above the planet. Oneness had replaced the twoness by a fusing of my higher and lower self. I physically felt the splitting of being. The human being was on the planet, feet firmly planted on the ground, while my highest self was witnessing the universe and infinity of space. Once I focused my physical form back on the ground, the doors of perception merged into a clear reflection of my authentic self. The *Now-ist* I became was the ultimate cleansing of the doors.

What happened next was the presentation of the doorway itself. When I simply looked down at the carpeted floor beneath me one day, that flash of enlightenment was there in image and formation. It was as if before this clear image presented itself to me, I was, "seeing all things thru' narrow chinks of his cavern," as Blake states. To me, it felt like I walked in a cavern and noticed an ancient symbol or hieroglyphic. This was the universal symbol that explained so much in one seemingly normal image. I noticed the cross first, which was in the catholic design, *catholic* means universal. Next, all four points of the cross looked like human figures with arms out-stretched. The four beings all hovered above a light source that was a circle like the earth. I looked again and noticed the four beings also looked like the rays of light coming out of the light source. That is when it hit me. "**I AM** the light of the world." This simple symbol was the clear doorway of perception and the mirrored passage to the infinite. I saw myself in the symbol as the light of the world. Another symbolic meaning I noticed was the horizontal line the cross made intersected with the vertical line. The horizontal line represents chronological or linear time and the vertical line embodies divine time. When I looked at the *Now-ist* symbol, I noticed the center had an explosion of light. This expressed the point in presence where you cross chronological time with divine time and enter the Now. When you are fully aware of this one single moment in time and all of your being-ness is focused there, you have cleansed the doors of perception and entered the infinite and timeless Now.

As I stood tall and looked down at the carpeted floor again, I could Now see that all of the *Now-ist* symbols are perfectly interconnected to one another. They are the representation to my awareness that we are each and every one of us the light of the world. God tells Moses at the burning bush his name is *I am that I am.* As I look at the symbols before me, I see God is in all of us, as Us. The famous quotation by Elizabeth Barrett Browning makes so much sense to me. As I contemplate the unaware beings she describes, "Earth's crammed with heaven, and every common bush afire with God, but only he who sees takes off his shoes; the rest sit round and pluck blackberries." People walk on these symbols everyday and never have the awareness of being that is with them always. It is my intention to awaken this in you, the reader, and gift you this truth. When you focus on the *Now-ist* symbol this time around, notice how it looks like a compass. It has four points of direction, only they all lead you to one place... the only place you should always travel... the journey without distance... the Now... for we are all... One-Now-Won.

CHAPTER 17

THE JOURNEY JOURNAL

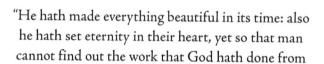

"He hath made everything beautiful in its time: also
he hath set eternity in their heart, yet so that man
cannot find out the work that God hath done from
the beginning even to the end" (Ecclesiastes 3:11).

L ife is the journey of the heart. We take our strides and steps toward
a faith-filled future that is our soul's desire. Most unknowingly, we
travel and journey in a direction that is guided by hopes and dreams. This
is indeed an adventure of will and persistence. However, many human
beings feel as if the world just gives them what it will and fate is the force
that ultimately decides. I am here to tell you, there is something else: a force
that is always with you. A sign from the divine that is here to show you the
way. A light for your path on your journey! Synchronicity is that force and
that light. *Spiritual bread crumbs* are left for you to follow home. It is time
for you to make that connection to the divine events that are pointing you
in the right direction. In my life these synchronistic events have always
amazed and inspired me. About ten years ago, I decided to keep track of
these spiritual bread crumbs in what I call a *Journey Journal*. The following
are real-life accounts of the synchronicity that strengthens my life's journey.
My hope is that it will inspire you as well to take notice of the events that
reveal themselves to you for you.

The Now-ist Symbol is Revealed

"Imagination is more important than knowledge," Einstein said. I have truly experienced that. Since I have been blessed with the power of Now, I have used a visualization technique in which I see myself floating above the earth, arms stretched out, and seeing the globe below me. This in kind transports me into a state of no mind. The only feeling is the Holy Spirit and the attraction of the positive blessed energies. One day I was walking down our hall at El Escorial, the condominium complex that we live in. I looked down at the carpet and was amazed to see a symbol that looked just like what I imagined and contemplated for myself when I am hovering above the planet. This was the very beginning of the Now-ist symbol and the impetus for the entire book that you are reading Now!

GiGi and the Balloons

My daughter Gigi and I walked into a grocery store one winter afternoon. Outside, there was a homeless lady asking for change. Gigi gave her a dollar and the lady said, "thank you." We finished our shopping and the check-out attendant offered, "Hey, we are giving good little girls two Valentine's Day helium balloons today." The cashier did not know what Gigi had done outside the store. I explained to Gigi the "Give to Live" feelings and how the universe works. I also taught her about the law of attraction and that gratitude is the greatest multiplier. What a great lesson for our little girl. She now has real-life experience with this key precept of living a God-realized life.

Give and It Will Be Given to You

On March 14th, I found myself feeling the need to donate to many causes that presented themselves to me that day. It started with a friend asking for a donation for the Arthritis Walk. Then, I felt compelled to donate to Japan's recovery efforts from the massive tsunami. Next, my "Nana's Fund" had not had any recent donations that I knew of, so I donated to my dearest Nana. Finally, I spoke with Pa and discovered that my Uncle Gil had a heart attack and was in need of help. The entire 24 hour period, I did not think of, what's in this for me. The power of God and love showed me the speed of Jesus' promise, "Give, and it will be given to you. A good measure, pressed down, shaken together and running over, will be poured into your lap. For with the measure you use, it will be measured to you." The very next day, I received two buyers and wrote two offers on the same day! This has never happened to me before working in real estate. I learned a wonderful lesson that day. I am forever thankful for blessings and the power of LOVE!

The Connecting Power of Love

I had been so excited for my buddy Darin to make it on the television singing contest called the X Factor. He had auditioned with me in Los Angeles just weeks prior. He did not get a call back from that audition. He was inspired to fly to Seattle to try out again. After his bold effort in Seattle, it inspired me to think of doing the same. I was feeling a little down, this being the last stop for the X Factor auditions. What is God's will for me? My wife and daughter went to the playground for a couple of hours. I did not know when they were going to come back. I grabbed my cross necklace and knelt beside the bed. I prayed for a sign to show me what to do. "Whatever it may be Lord, I am ready for your answer." One second after finishing my prayer, Gigi came bursting through the front door screaming, "Daddy, Daddy, Daddy!" She came over to the bed and I helped her jump up and down a few times as we usually played. She then did the most incredible thing. She got really close to my face and just like Nana, my greatest fan of my singing use to do, tapped me on the forehead three times. She said, "That was from Nana." I looked at her in absolute amazement! The Lord and my dear Nana answered my prayer in the fastest time I have ever experienced in my entire life. My flight was booked and I was off to perform for the judges in Seattle. Thanks be to God.

I Am is Always the Champ

I just felt the flow and divine energy of the miracle that is ours if we feel and believe, I AM that I AM the conquering presence in the NOW! I had been reading Dr. Wayne Dyer's, *Wishes Fulfilled*. He speaks of I AM, (the name of God). I used this proclamation over and over again while in the throws of the Santa Barabara City Golf Championship, which I WON! I visualized the Now, being above the world and saw each shot with clarity and power. I was in the Now almost every single shot of the tournament. I had never broken an 80 score in any of the previous five years of attempting to make the tournament cut. My focus and clarity with every shot was an experience that I had never felt before. Too often I had been focusing on the end score, which takes away from the shot at hand. This time, the I AM presence carried me high above all the other golfers. I had an eight shot lead going into the penultimate hole of the three day competition. Yet, then my focus was temporarily lost on the 17th hole, my mind and fear-based old habits snuck in. However, after that quadruple bogey, I bounced back and regained my I AM awareness and WON the biggest tournament in the city by four shots!

Thinking from the End... Not About the End

I was blessed to list a condo unit for sale at my home setting, El Escorial. I had spent six years contacting an absentee owner about selling. She only gave me five days to sell the unit. I took the listing without a doubt and told my wife, "I will sell this unit." I got an offer from a neighbor just two days into the listing. The offer was $20,000 short of the asking price. The seller countered back at full price. The agent said that was a deal breaker. After hanging up the phone, I entered the NOW. Above the world, I imaged the scene: the closing of the escrow, hugging the new owner, then shaking the agent's hand in congratulations. The next day, I paid many things forward. Generosity was in my heart and the point of my attraction. I helped homeless people and was just walking into Costco to purchase Christmas gifts for three less fortunate children in Santa Barbara. My phone rang and it was the agent completely shocked. His buyer had agreed to the full price and she was happy to pay it. Thoughts are things!

Feeling is the Secret

January 8th, 2011 was the day that my beloved Nana made her transition back to spirit. It was nighttime as I walking out to the garage with a heavy mind. I looked up to the stars and imagined myself above the world. For about a week, my mind had been taken over by negative feelings. I was thinking about the fact that I had three vacancies in my rental properties. Time was running out to fill all three by the end of the month. I looked up at the stars and with great feeling directed my heart and emotions to imagining the units filling. I saw each condo occupied with a happy tenant, one-by-one. I felt incredibly free and definitive about the issue. I walked up stairs and looked over at the clock; it read 11:11, the number of synchronicity. In just three days from that fate-filled night, all three units were leased out. I was thankfully in awe to be in sync and total alignment with the universe. I had three vacancies and there were three families in need of residence. I know my Nana is my Guardian Angel and she inspires me to be the best version of me always. I had just learned a great lesson about faith and "Feeling is the Secret," as Neville Goddard brilliantly states in his book by the same title.

Sufficiently Desired...

One night as I laid in bed, I was wondering why I had not had any showings for awhile for two great rental units. This reminded me of a passage from the book *Zorba the Greek*, "That which has not been manifested has not been sufficiently desired." I imagined a new tenant in each unit and did so in the Now from above the world, as I do. The next morning, I received two calls, one for each unit! The first prospect was clairvoyant and said she heard a voice last night tell her out loud, "Por La Mar." I shared with her that I am a Now-ist and believe in living in the moment with our power of divinity. She was excited and said she would take the unit. We are all connected. We must consciously connect to manifest our desires.

Billy... Are you Ready? Now-Ex-ist

I had a new tenant that moved into the condo directly above ours. Her name was Annie, an in-tune with energy type of person. She met me for the first time and said, "You are on the fast track of consciousness and enlightenment." She also noticed a bright light around me that she said was my Nana. One day when I was walking over to our tennis courts to sign up to play, I was thinking about the feeling of hovering above the world.

I thought, *How great would it be to simulate that experience in an IMAX Theater? You could have cold air blowing on you as if you were above the world in space.* I then switched my thinking to what Annie said about her seeing me as a great teacher, "Put your seat belt on because you are in for a ride." I finished that thought as I opened the door to the building. There on the lobby table I saw a flyer that said, "BILLY ARE YOU READY?" This title was written above a picture of planet earth! I once read that when you align with God and your higher purpose, God sends you greater beings to aid you in your journey. I feel that this was a wonderful and amazing example of staying awake and watching the signs. Thank you my Heavenly Father and my guardian angel Nana.

G.O.L.F... *Life Lessons the Hard Way*

Saturday of the Santa Barbara Golf Club Championship, I was awakened the "hard way." Standing on the far side of the fairway on hole 12, I was looking down the hill toward the green, contemplating my next shot. Out of "nowhere," I was struck on the back of the head from someone's errant drive from the 14th tee. I lost vision for a couple of seconds and was rolling around on the ground in pain. My first thought was, *I must have been hit by a rock or a bullet.* After sometime, Tyrell Bennett, a new friend and plumber I had hired recently, drove over to me. He was sincerely sorry and not quite sure if it was his ball that hit me. After searching for his ball and not finding it, he knew that it was his ball that hit me. Ironically, I was paired with Tyrell the next day of the tournament.

I know that all events are synchronistic and accidents are vibrational alignments with God's universe. I spoke with him in detail. It turned out, he shot an eight on hole 12, a seven on 13, and when he arrived at the 14th tee, he was very mad and decided to take it out on the ball. I know that if I had been in the "Now" and completely present, I would have not attracted this outcome.

It had been a few years since I had seen my synchronistic-friend Tyrell Bennett. Then one day, I was at a local plumbing supply store buying a toilet for my wife's bathroom. The toilet I decided on had to be ordered. As I stood at the counter talking to the sales clerk, guess who walks up beside me. Tyrell Bennett! We exchanged a big hug and he proceeded to give me his contractor's discount on the toilet; he then offered to install it for free. After this magnanimous display, his tale of hitting me in the back of the head from 250 yards filled the plumbing store and all within ear-shot were amazed.

A Wink from Nana

October 9th, 2013. Gigi walked from her room to meet me at the front door on our way to school. As she passed the living room, all the smoke alarms and CO2 alarms in the house started beeping at the same time. I walked over to each one of them and smelled the house for smoke, or something that might have set them off. Once Gigi and I left the house and shut the door, they all stopped! I then knew that is was NANA saying "hi" and giving us her love and presence. On the way to school, I asked Gigi if she had said something or had looked at Nana's picture on her wall. She said that she winked at Nana's picture. Nana taught our girl to wink when she was only a couple of years old!

Nana the "Pepper Puppy"

On June 8th, 2014, I was continuing my search for Gigi's early birthday gift. My wife and I had decided that it was time for our family to have a puppy. I looked, asked, and researched for a solid month and no puppy. I was talking to a puppy trainer who was referred to me by a friend. She said to search the internet. I searched for Yorkies in the area and clicked on the first add. It showed a cute little Yorkie. I emailed and then texted the owner about the pup. She called me back and stated that she had a couple of puppies. One was very expensive and the other one was sweet and lovable. I asked her to send me a picture. The picture had a name on it. The puppy's name was "Nana!" I knew this was to be our new family member. When I asked where the puppy was located, she said Littlerock, California. I told her that we would be coming back from Vegas on Monday, June 23rd (this is one day after my Nana's birthday!) and asked if we could come pick up Nana, our new puppy, then. She said that the puppy might not be available by then. I decided it was fate and no matter what, I would have faith and know that this lil' pup was meant for our Gi. The morning that we left for

Las Vegas, the time was 5:30 a.m. when my wife and I walked out the door. I glanced at the newspaper on the front door step of our neighbor's across the hall. The headline read, "PUPPY DOE" which means girl puppy! I love the way life works when you are in the NOW!

Life is a Cakewalk

One afternoon, I was spinning music as the DJ at the cakewalk for my daughter's school spring carnival. Gigi really wanted to win a cake. She had tried to win a cake ten times, but to no avail. The cakewalk cost one ticket per game. She only had three tickets left and her frustration level was high. Completely discouraged, she walked up to the DJ both where I was orchestrating the music. I told her, "This time I want you to hold the cake in your hands. Smell the cake, taste the cake, and feel all of this in your imagination Now! You have to believe more than the other fifteen people playing the game that you will win!" After about a minute of walking her through this exercise, I asked her to give it one more try. With God as my witness, she won her cake that very next round. She was beaming from the hidden power that she discovered that warm spring day. The high was partially the sugar rush too.

Better Than a Hole-in-One

The greatest "GOLF" (Go On Life's Feelings) birthday gift that I ever received was given on May 6th, 2015. Desa, my love, decided to take me to our local municipal golf course for nine holes on my birthday. I showed her on the ninth hole my ritual. She was emotionally moved to see that after fifteen years, the tree that I carved the letters BAD on, was still there. (This stood for Billy And Desa.) She traced the letters to make it deeper. I told her that each time I walked off the eighth green, I touched the BAD and then tapped on a metal water drum just after the tree. After recounting my ritual, I proceeded to hit a soaring tee shot about 270 yards. I had 242 yards to the pin. I gripped down on a three-wood and then felt the rush of hitting a masterful shot. I tracked the ball with my eyes, as it was heading right at the red flag on the green. As I walked up with my wife, I could not see my ball. Once I was about thirty yards from the green, my heart started to race.

I crept up to the hole and saw that once-in-a-lifetime site of the ball resting at the bottom of the cup. I let out a massive shout of joy. An Albatross! My love took a movie with her iPhone of the spectacular event so we could share this wonderful gift. "When you feel like you have everything you need, you get everything you want."

Pole Vaulting over Mouse Turds

God bless my dearest Dr. Wayne Dyer. He has inspired me for a decade. One day, I was listening to his *Change your Thoughts - Change your Life* program on a PBS special. Through this wonderful translation, he explains the Tao Te Jing. In it, he uses this unique expression, "Don't pole vault over mouse turds." To me this quotation means- to not make a big deal about little things. A literal connection to me, my junior year of high school, I placed second in the pole vault at the state meet. Flash forward, I was dealing with a rather negative tenant at a property. She was making the biggest deal out of dusty blinds. We had the property professionally cleaned just days ago for her. I found the most opportune time to interject into the conversation Dr. Wayne's words. "Don't pole vault over mouse turds." Although she did not take it well, she would probably later think about it and perhaps review her nit-picking. I left the house shortly thereafter. When I started my car to drive away, the six hour *Change your Thoughts - Change your Life* audio book instantly started up with exactly Dr. Wayne stating, "Not to pole vault over mouse turds!" Synchronicity again! I said a prayer out-loud and thanked Wayne for being everywhere!

A Model Account of Synchronicity

While getting a hair cut in my dear friend Cinder's chair at her salon, she asked me about my early modeling experience. I recounted the feelings and emotions of my first job. I felt myself slip back into the actual studio and remembered the two female stylists and photographer. When I told her the punch line of the "banana in my briefs," she really cracked up. The most incredible part of this story is what happened the following day. My nieces, Katie and Claire, were celebrating their 13th birthdays in Spokane with the family. Brother Gib was visiting with our sister Jen. She was showing him all the old pictures she had of our family. Gib proceeded to send me a text message along with a picture that said, "Compliments of Aunt Jen. LOL!" He had taken a picture of my first modeling job, an underwear advertisement from the newspaper. I instantly texted it to my friend Cinder's and she freaked out. Synchronicity is an "under-statement!"

Synchronicity Never Misses a Beat

My bandmate Kirstin and I were hired to play a gig in Camarillo with our musical friend, Allie. Between sets, I was speaking with them about the meaning and examples of Synchronicity. Neither of them had ever heard of the term. They were kind of looking at me with glazed-over eyes. When I finished with my "Synchro-Stories," about a minute passed and a text rang my phone from my wife. It said, "Synchronicity!" I instantly showed it to Allie and Candy. She also sent a video that was of our daughter Gigi playing her guitar for her friend Lauren. Des said in her video, "This is Synchronicity. Daddy is playing music and so is Gigi!" Allie and Candy responded, "Wow that is amazing!" Writer, Stuart Chase, illuminates faith in his words, "For those who believe, no proof is necessary. For those who don't believe, no proof is possible."

Thoughts are Things

One summer day, Gigi wanted to go to the movies. She requested her friend Lauren to come as well. She asked me many times. I finally texted Lauren's mom and asked her to come. I did not tell Gigi that I contacted Lauren's mom. I decided to give her some inspirational tools instead. While we were standing under the marquee at the Fiesta Five Movie Theatre, I asked her to close her eyes and imagine what it would look like to have Lauren show up at the front of the theater and get out of her mom's car. I asked her to imagine how she felt emotionally, what she saw as the expression on Lauren's face, when she stepped out of the car. I already knew that Lauren was coming, but Gigi did not. I wanted to give her an experience with imagination manifestation. She did this visualizing exercise as I requested. Approximately one minute later, 103.3 The Vibe radio station's van pulled up in front of the marquee and stopped while recording with their camera. The DJ said, "We are live to 100,000 listeners right Now!" He then asked Gigi to come to the van because he had free tickets to give-away for Hurricane Harbor at Six Flags Magic Mountain! Her eyes were popping out when he handed her the tickets. Gigi was taught an amazing lesson that day- that when in a state of imagination, things come to you. Just a few minutes later, Lauren's mom pulled up right in front of the marquee and Gigi's belief soared to even greater heights! She was keenly inspired by her own power. Imagination is the most powerful gift our good Lord has given us.

Butterfly's Never Doubt

Entering the driveway to Glen Annie Golf Course, I was listening to *The Power of Intention*. As Dr. Wayne was speaking about synchronicity and the people who believe, I then had the thought, "Isn't it amazing how he continually keeps showing up to me in the Monarch butterfly form?" Synchronistically and precisely as those two ideas came together, a Monarch butterfly glanced off the entire length of my windshield! I just love how he keeps showing up for me in this shape and form. I am reminded of one of his favorite messages from *A Course in Miracles*, "If you knew who walked beside you, on this journey you have chosen, you could never experience fear or doubt again."

CHAPTER 18

NOW... WHERE DO I GO?

---❦---

"And now, go, write it before them on a tablet
and inscribe it in a book, that it may be for
the time to come as a witness forever."

— Isaiah 30:8

There comes a time in every person's life, the existential question is asked of oneself: "Who Am I?" I maintain that every sentient being on the planet is programmed to ask this question. It relates directly to the truth of our oneness. After all, we are on a journey seeking to get back home. What I find most interesting about the question, "Who Am I?" is the fact that the answer is in the question, similar to the anagram Now-Won, which is the word NOW spelled backwards. This reminds us that when we are in the Now, we have Won our presence in any of life's moments. *Who Am I*, when read in reverse, is *I AM*. We know the name of God is I AM, so who you are is God as well. You are the I AM that I AM. Hence, when you ask yourself the question, "Who am I?" you instantly have the answer. Yes, the simplicity here can be mind-blowing. Consider the billions of awe-inspiring creations of God. Just look at the night sky on a clear evening. The billions of stars and planets out there. We all take most blessings for granted. Stop and stare at a wild flower. Jesus reminds us:

> Consider the lilies of the field, how they grow: they neither
> toil nor spin, yet I tell you, even Solomon in all his glory
> was not arrayed like one of these. But if God so clothes

the grass of the field, which today is alive and tomorrow is
thrown into the oven, will he not much more clothe you,
O you of little faith? (Matthew 6:25-34).

In essence, He is telling us not to be anxious or worry. All is as it
should be; have faith. Furthermore, William Blake also delivers the Now-ist
teaching in his all-encompassing poem:

To see a World in a Grain of Sand
And a Heaven in a Wild Flower,
Hold Infinity in the palm of your hand
And Eternity in an hour,
We are led to Believe a Lie, When we see not Through
the Eye,
Which was Born in a Night, to perish in a Night,
When the Soul Slept in Beams of Light.

"To every thing there is a season, and a time to every purpose under the
heaven" (Ecclesiastes 3:1). Although, the illusion of time drives us daily in
a race against the clock, you have learned throughout this book about the
only power you truly have: The Now. When you entered this embodiment,
it occurred precisely when it was meant to happen. The timing and plan of
the creator is evident in all of nature. "I am the beginning and the end. The
Alpha and the Omega." You are the most precious of all of God's creations.
After all, God became us, so that we may become God. You come into
the world as God and you leave the world as God. When you can shift
your awareness of being to the miraculous You Are, everything becomes
quite evident. Albert Einstein with his powerful wisdom explained this
transmutation, "There are only two ways to live your life. One is as though
nothing is a miracle. The other is as though everything is a miracle." It
does not matter what faith tradition you have been raised or are currently
practicing. When you can look in the mirror and know that God is staring
back at you, this is the miracle that needs to reign in your life.

When you finally know and feel that you are God, you use life's
circumstance to direct you on your path in alignment with the creative
source that you are. The power you have is like a self guidance system;

it is called synchronicity. Deepak Chopra explains, "Synchronicity is the awareness of the usefulness for your benefit of a person or object that directs you on your path." This journey we take back to God, empowered by our awareness, is inevitable. The signs and symbols are all around us and in us. The Now-ist symbol, you learned, is in the shape of a cross. One horizontal line representing *chronological time* and the vertical line representing *divine time*. The point at which these two lines cross is the Now. The Now-ist symbol shows the explosion of light at this moment of intersection. Imagine your body, Now. Lay on the floor with your arms out-stretched to your sides. Bring your legs together flat on the ground. You have just created a cross or your own Now-ist symbol. Now consider the intersecting point on your body, as you lay on the ground in the shape of the Now-ist symbol. The point at which your outstretched arms and head-to-toe body-line meet is your heart. This is the center of your universe. This is the power center of your entire being. The heart is your faith-feeling organ. It rules your body, mind, and soul. This is your Now-ist awakening. You are "the light of the world." Your heart is that light. You have traveled so far, only to find that you took a journey without distance. You are here, you are Now, you are Home.

Our doubt about the truth, of whom is staring back at you, once you look into the mirror with awareness, can be earth-shaking. When that feeling comes, go to the signs that have synchronistically lead you to this point in your life. Pay attention to all the *Spiritual Bread Crumbs* that have led you to this moment of awakening. Most importantly, rest in the Sabbath, which means to come to the end. When you can relinquish all mind-made thoughts and fear-based fallacies, you will come to the end. The knowing will come to you. Offer no resistance to the feeling that is rising up within you. "Be still, and know that I am God" (Psalm 46:10).

You have to look at the world and your life with the eyes of a child. Bewilderment and a deep curiosity will keep you fresh and young. Children instinctively live in the Now. At the core of a child is a Now-ist. They live on the feelings of freedom and no mind. That child in us never has to grow up, spiritually speaking. Realize, that which is real never changes. Our soul is always young and vibrant. You have to live as a child-like "Bi-Terrestrial" in your wondrous imagination above the planet with your feet firmly on the ground. Of course, the challenges will come. Our relationships can be some of the most trying experiences of our journey. However, when you learn to "Clean and Clear" your energy, the Relation-Ships you travel with will sail through the rough waters, while the winds of change will push you to that safe harbor. Eventually, these vessels we traverse the vast planet with need reminding of the "dis-ease" that can occur from traveling. We need to be like the water we arrived here from, soft and yielding, flexible yet powerful. Remembering the "Real-State" we are in, changeless, yet ever changing. We need to live in that duality of life and our life's situation. The realization of our true self, that is omnipotent, omniscient, and omnipresent. We need to be complete in our being-ness and not need to focus on a "goal" to make us fulfilled or satisfied. Contentment will be the feeling that reigns over the heart in this, our journey home. A Now-ist thinks not about the end, but from the end, of a desire or inspirational act. No goals are needed, just a soulful awareness. You need to die before you die. One must die to the past every single moment in total surrender to this present feeling of Oneness, which is our Now-ist truth. This truth is closer than near and sooner than Now. We are infinite and we are God. "We are not our bodies, our possessions, or our careers; who we are is divine love, and that is infinite" teaches our Dr. Wayne Dyer. Our infinity and our divinity is lived each and every moment in content awareness. A Now-ist sits at the throne of thy heart, content and pure in being. You are Now-Won in imagination, and the I AM presence is all that you are.

Acknowledgement

My heart feels love and appreciation for the oneness that has connected my life to the following angels. These individuals have inspired me to create and become The Now-ist! I am blessed by God to have this life and by union with the divine spirits bring these inspirations to you. To my soul-mate Desa, I am forever in love with you and the joy you give me. Thank you, Wifey, and prolific writer and golfing buddy, Mike Bowker, for editing this book. It would not have been complete without you. To my sunshine GiGi, you make my heart sing and fill my life with the greatest of gifts, being your Daddy. To my incredible Pa, my life would not be what it is today without your love and guidance. I love you Momma for bringing me into this world. To Cindy, Mindy, Wendy, brother Gib, and Jenny, the love I feel because of your collective hearts has shaped my very being and taught me that "Family is love in a bunch." I am so blessed to have Neal D aka "The Moment Man" as a kindred spirit and brother from another mother. Thank you Ricker and Marcia Pecel for loving me and supporting my dreams. To my dear Perky, aka Loretta McClure, your light and spirit shines on all of us. To Dr. Wayne Dyer, Neville Goddard, Prince, and my Nana, aka Mildred Mandarino- the "Faithful Four." Your inspiration and angelic guidance has filled my life and these pages with divine love.

ABOUT THE AUTHOR

Billy Mandarino lives in Santa Barbara, California with his wonderful wife, Desa Marie, and their incredible daughter, Gianna. Billy claims that he fell in love with his wife and Santa Barbara simultaneously. This is the magical city that brought them together more than twenty five years ago.

The inspiration and truth Billy Mandarino presents in The Now-ist is a life-changing creation. Not only for the author, but more importantly, the readers and souls he serves. With a spiritual hunger that is never quenched, Billy dives deep into the essence of us all. He takes the common place and makes it "real."

Growing up in a five-sibling, multiple-divorces family, with all its dynamic layers and change, initially shaped the author's spirituality. Transformed by various religious practices and study through-out his life, he has recognized via life experience, the treasures that reside within us all to be discovered. It is his ultimate calling to light the way, for the ones called to the same magnetic energy that inspired him to write this very book.

Billy has a presence that is felt in his writing and penetrates even deeper in person. Most of his life, people are drawn to him for advice and direction in all areas of life. He is incessantly of service to others and has recognized that the inspiration to write The Now-ist is his highest calling. He feels uniquely blessed to share his light with millions around the globe.

For more information to go deeper into The Now-ist teachings and see/ hear Billy live- visit www.BillyMandarino.com

CPSIA information can be obtained
at www.ICGtesting.com
Printed in the USA
BVHW07*0012290918
528605BV00001B/3/P